IRAN:
WHERE
MASS
MURDERERS
RULE

The 1988 Massacre of 30,000 Political Prisoners and the Continuing Atrocities

A Publication of the ῀   ϵ OF IRAN
VE Office

D0814067

First published in 2017 by National Council of Resistance of Iran - U.S. Representative Office (NCRI-US), 1747 Pennsylvania Ave., NW, Suite 1125, Washington, DC 20006

ISBN-10 (hard cover): 1-944942-12-2
ISBN-13 (hard cover): 978-1-944942-12-0

ISBN-10 (paperback): 1-944942-10-6
ISBN-13 (paperback): 978-1-944942-10-6

ISBN-10 (eBook): 1-944942-11-4
ISBN-13 (eBook): 978-1-944942-11-3

Library of Congress Control Number: 2017961491

Library of Congress Cataloging-in-Publication Data

National Council of Resistance of Iran - U.S. Representative Office.

Iran: Where Mass Murderers Rule, The 1988 Massacre of 30,000 Political Prisoners and the Continuing Atrocities

Iran. 2. Human rights. 3. Massacre. 4. Middle East. 5. United Nations

First Edition: December 2017

Printed in the United States of America

These materials are being distributed by the National Council of Resistance of Iran-U.S. Representative Office. Additional information is on file with the Department of Justice, Washington, D.C.

TABLE OF CONTENTS

FOREWORD

This book presented by the National Council of Resistance of Iran addresses one of the darkest stains on the recent history of mankind and yet a stain that has neither been acknowledged nor discussed by the international community. The events themselves make for compelling reading, and the NCRI's account lays bare the truth about an incredibly deadly series of crimes carried out nearly three decades ago. But more importantly, its publication is timely because those responsible for Iran's "summer of blood" have never been held accountable; justice has never been served. The criminals remain in power, and their crimes are ongoing.

The events of 1988 are clear. Ayatollah Ruhollah Khomeini's "fatwa" order to execute leftists and members of the principal opposition movement, the Mujahedin-e Khalq (MEK) was implemented with deadly efficiency. Over a period of just five months, the commissions or "death committees" established to carry out the executions rounded up tens of thousands of political prisoners. The executions took place in many prisons across Iran. Most victims were political prisoners, including an unknown number of "prisoners of conscience," who had already served a number of years in prison. Many of the executed had been tried and sentenced to prison terms during the early 1980s, many for non-violent offences such as distributing newspapers and leaflets, taking part in demonstrations, or collecting funds for prisoners' families. Many of them had been students in their teens or early twenties at the time of their arrest. After "trials" that lasted only minutes, in total, nearly 30,000 Iranian citizens were executed as part of the regime's campaign to wipe out its opposition.

Since 1988, the Iranian regime has worked hard to cover up these horrors. The locations of the mass grave sites remain largely unknown and the public is banned from visiting the ones that have been uncovered. The regime's relentless propaganda campaign has painted the MEK victims as villains. An open letter to Amnesty International from the Permanent Mission of the Islamic Republic of Iran to the UN in New York in February 1989 stated: "Indeed, authorities of the Islamic Republic of Iran have always denied the existence of any political executions, but that does not contradict other subsequent statements which have confirmed that spies and terrorists have been executed." (UN document A/44/153, 28 February 1989)

The August 2016 emergence of a tape recording of Ayatollah Hossein-Ali Montazeri, Khomeini's designated successor in 1988, condemning the massacre during a meeting of high-ranking officials finally made it impossible for the regime to deny the massacre. In the recording, during an August 1988 meeting, Montazeri states that the massacre was "the greatest crime committed under the Islamic Republic" and that the "mass executions without trials, particularly as it relates to prisoners and captives… definitely over time will favor them and the world will condemn us." The fact that senior officials of the regime—all of whom continue to serve today—were present at this meeting proves their direct culpability in these heinous crimes.

Members of the "death committees" established in 1988 remain high ranking government officials today, including the current justice minister, Alireza Avayi. Iran continues to use public executions as a means of punishing political and religious prisoners, and leads the world in per capita executions. Further, it is the only nation in the world that still executes juveniles.

The families of the victims in Iran deserve closure and justice, which cannot be achieved without an investigation into the brutality perpetrated by the regime. The NCRI's book walks us through the events of 1988, and into present day Iran, where those responsible for the horrific crimes of

After "trials" that lasted only minutes, in total, nearly 30,000 Iranian citizens were executed as part of the regime's campaign to wipe out its opposition.

1988 continue to rule by violence, intimidation and execution. If the global community is indeed committed to upholding justice and human rights, we must lay bare their crimes, and demand that those who violate international law on such a deadly scale be held responsible for their actions.

J. Kenneth Blackwell

Former United States Ambassador
United Nations Human Rights Commission

PREFACE

Late in July 1988, as the war with Iraq was ending in a truculent truce, prisons in Iran crammed with government opponents suddenly went into lockdown. All family visits were cancelled, televisions and radios switched off and newspapers discontinued. Prisoners were kept in their cells, disallowed exercise or trips to the infirmary. The only permitted visitation was from a delegation, turbaned and bearded, which came in government BMWs and Mercedes to outlying jails: a religious judge, a public prosecutor, and an intelligence chief. Before them were paraded, briefly and individually, almost every prisoner (and there were thousands of them) who had been jailed for adherence to the Mujahedin-e Khalq (MEK). The delegation had but one question for these young men and women (most of them detained since 1981 merely for taking part in street protests or possession of "political" reading material), and although they did not know it, on the answer their life would depend. Those who by their answer evinced any continuing affiliation with the MEK were blindfolded and ordered to join a conga-line that led straight to the gallows. They were hung from cranes, four at a time, or in groups of six from ropes hanging from the stage in an assembly hall; some were taken to army barracks at night, directed to make their wills and then shot by firing squad. Their bodies were doused with disinfectant, placed packed in refrigerated trucks and buried by night in mass graves. Months later their families, desperate for information about their children or their partners, would be handed a plastic bag with their few possessions. They would be refused any information about the location of the graves and ordered never to mourn them in public. By mid-August 1988, thousands of prisoners had been killed in this manner by the state – without trial, without appeal and utterly without mercy.

That was my judicial conclusion about what happened in Iranian prisons in 1988, based on evidence and interviews. And of course, the regime having killed the MEK members, then went on and killed thousands whose religious views or non-religious views were regarded as atheistic. Families still are not allowed to know where the bodies of their loved ones are buried. This too is contrary to international law, yet still the "Mullahs without Mercy" (the title of my book about these atrocities) deny their people the right to grieve.

Without any reasonable doubt, these are crimes against humanity. It has been a crime to kill prisoners for over 400 years. The rules during the wars in Europe were always that a prisoner once surrendered could not be killed without trial and could not be tortured. In my opinion, the state of Iran has committed four exceptionally serious breaches of *jus cogens* rules of international law which entail both state responsibility and individual accountability for war crimes and crimes against humanity:

1 The arbitrary killing of thousands of male and female prisoners pursuant to a *fatwa* that held them collectively responsible for "steadfast" allegiance to the Mojahedin, notwithstanding that they had been in prison and *hors de combat* for years, serving fixed term sentences for relatively minor offences. This was not the execution of a lawful sentence, because there was no trial, no charge and no criminal act other than adhering to a particular ideological group. The right to life, guaranteed by customary international law, by treaties to which Iran is a party and by the Geneva Conventions, was quite deliberately and barbarically breached, and all who bear international law responsibility for this mass murder should be prosecuted. An obligation to prosecute may also arise from the Genocide Convention, since the reason why MEK members were condemned as *moharebs* ("warriors against God") and exterminated was that they had adopted a version of Islam which differed from that upheld by the State.

2 The second wave of apostate killings was also a breach of the right to life, as well as the right to religious freedom. Prisoners were executed for a crime of conscience in that their only offence was to refuse to adopt the religious beliefs, prayers and rituals of the state. They were not, as the government later alleged, spies or terrorists or prison rioters. They were executed to rid a theocratic state of ideological enemies in post-war circumstances that could not possibly give rise to a defense of necessity or to any other defense.

3 **The beatings inflicted on leftist women and on other men who were regarded as capable of religious compliance satisfied the definition of torture, which is absolutely prohibited even if it is consonant with national law.** The only object of the beatings was to break their will and their spirit and to make them more amenable to the state's version of Islamic governance.

4 **Finally, the rights to know where close relatives have been buried and to mourn their deaths, have been and still are being denied by the state.** What is being denied, almost three decades after the deaths, is the right of parents, spouses and siblings to manifest their feelings of devotion in respect of the memory of a family member. Further, the refusal to identify mass graves implicitly involves a refusal to allow DNA testing (which has proven reliable in war crimes investigations as a means of identifying the remains in mass graves) and, in consequence, the prevention of a proper burial.

The individuals against whom there is a *prima facie* case for prosecution for crimes against humanity, torture, genocide and war crimes, are those "who bear most responsibility" in the chain of command. The members of the Death Committee are well known, as are the senior prison officials who organized and authorized the executions, and no doubt those Revolutionary Guards who acted as hangmen, firing squad members and gravediggers can also be identified. Different ministries would have had to give approvals and directions, most importantly the Ministry of Information whose officials conducted interrogations, set questionnaires and kept tabs on every prisoner. There is evidence that, at some prisons, warders were supplanted by Revolutionary Guards who carried out the killings.

A list of individuals can be identified to have been directly responsible for approving the death and torture sentences that they must or should have known to have been contrary to international law. On the well-known principle established by the Nuremberg case of US v Joseph Altstoeter and others (the "Justice Case" dramatized in the film Judgment at Nuremberg) judges who contribute to crimes committed in the guise of legal process cannot themselves escape prosecution: as the Nuremberg prosecution put it, "men of law can no more escape... responsibility by virtue of their judicial robes, than the General by his uniform." Moreover, in considering the complicity of professionals in crimes against humanity, there is no good reason to exclude diplomats who, knowing the truth, nonetheless lie about it to UN bodies to whom they owe a duty of frankness.

The situation in Iran today illustrates the consequences of impunity for crimes against humanity that have never been properly investigated or acknowledged. Some of the perpetrators remain in powerful positions in the judiciary and the state, whose Supreme Leader Ali Khamenei has called upon the Revolutionary Guards to use violence against peaceful protests with the support of Ayatollah Mesbah Yazdi, who threatens that "[a]nybody resisting against the ruling system will be broken."[1] Those staged television show trials of the 1980s, with televised "confessions" by leftist prisoners wracked by torture and fear for their families, re-emerged in 2009, this time featuring 'Green Movement reformists' confessing to participation in an international conspiracy devised by the US and the British Embassy in collaboration with the BBC, Twitter, Facebook, George Soros, Human Rights Watch and Amnesty International.

Evin prison, scene of mass murder in 1988, remains a brutal environment for blindfolded prisoners picked up for no more serious offence than attending student demonstrations or contacting NGOs concerned about human rights. There have been many casualties, and many ironic reminders of 1988, the year of impunity. The brutal treatment of Nazanin Ratcliffe, a charity worker sentenced to prison and parted from her baby on bogus spying charges, is just the latest case in point.

One of Grand Ayatollah Montazeri's very last acts was to call on Iranians to accord three days of mourning to Neda Agha-Soltan, the young woman student shot dead by forces loyal to Ahmadinejad; and to support other victims of the repressive state which he helped to create, but then came to condemn.

1   'Meet the Ayatollahs', *New Statesman*, 10 August 2009, 30.

It would be more sensible to impose sanctions for the crimes against humanity that occurred in 1988, so long as they go uninvestigated and unpunished, than it would to impose them for alleged moves towards uranium enrichment. Given the evidence of international crimes, including one which the 1948 Genocide Convention imposes a duty to investigate and punish without limit of time, the Security Council would be perfectly entitled under its Chapter VII powers to establish an international court with a prosecutor who can quickly collect the incriminatory evidence and obtain access to the relevant state witnesses and records. After all, the most reasonable objection to Iran developing nuclear power for peaceful purposes is the fact that it is a regime that has already granted itself impunity for mass murder, and may do so again.

Many obvious suspects are still alive and well. They were men in Khomeini's inner circle; ministers and diplomats who knew what was happening; judges who betrayed their calling by zealously sentencing prisoners to death and torture without trial; prison governors and intelligence officers who shepherded the blindfolded victims to the queue for the gallows. There are many more who have been identified by survivors and are listed on dissident websites. Although most of those judges and officials worked at Tehran's prisons, Evin and Gohardasht, where the main massacres took place, it is evident that there were hundreds and possibly thousands of prisoners killed in the provinces: Shiraz, Dezful, Tabriz, Qazvin, Arak, Khorramabad, Qom, Rasht, Esfahan, Mashhad, to name but ten local prisons. All would have had their trio of implacable judges, their willing executioners from among the prison officials and intelligence operatives and Revolutionary Guards.

In the annals of post-war horrors, the killings compare with the 1995 massacre at Srebrenica in terms of the vulnerability of the victims, and they exceed it when measured by the cold-blooded calculations made at the very pinnacle of state power. As long as the graves of the dead remain unmarked and relatives are forbidden from mourning, Iran will continue to contravene the rule of international law, which its leaders so brutally defied in 1988.

Geoffrey Robertson QC[2]

2   Geoffrey Robertson QC is founder and joint head of Doughty Street Chambers, London, serves as a Master of the Bench at the Middle Temple, a recorder, and visiting professor at Queen Mary University of London. He served as the first President and Appeal Judge in the UN War Crimes Court in Sierra Leone.

INTRODUCTION

It is an omnipresent phenomenon inherent to humankind. Throw a dart at any map; any small town, any large city, any community or organization—from a local chess club in a Parisian suburb to the NAACP offices in Baltimore, Maryland—one will find it: commemoration and observance of historical events or persons in an entity's past. Whether said acknowledgments are celebratory in nature—countries' raised glasses and belted anthems on Independence Day; or mournful—thousands of fresh flowers devouring the Armenian Genocide Memorial in Tsitsernakaberd each April; people are hardwired to pay homage to impactful figures and events of their past. Whether this past is a triumphant or failed one, a praiseworthy or shameful one, a progressive or destructive one, it is nevertheless remembered and reflected upon, whether on a personal, local, or national level.

No one denies, or contests man's urge to commemorate his past; the urge to capture and disseminate one's history is simply and universally accepted as a central trait that defines mankind. Nevertheless, this book was not bound to commemorate the 30,000 innocent men, women, and children who were hanged from cranes, swiftly shot dead, or executed by other grotesque means, across hundreds of cities in Iran in the relative blink of an eye in the summer of 1988. No, such a commemoration is not necessarily pressing, because such commemorations already exist. For the last 30 years, thousands of human rights and political activists, still-mourning friends and family members, as well as massacre survivors themselves, have dedicated their lives to publishing an extraordinary number of books, memoirs, articles, internationally recognized reports and exposés recounting the 1988 massacre in great detail.

Nowhere was this more evident than during the May 2017 presidential elections in Iran, when young and old, men and women, repeatedly used the opportunity to chant, "neither the Charlatan" (reference to incumbent president Hassan Rouhani), "nor the Murderer" (referencing his challenger, Ebrahim Raisi, among officials directly responsible for the largest case of state-ordered mass killings post-WW II)).

Ensuring the public never forgets the ideals, decisions, and fates of martyrs and tyrants alike, is instrumental in perpetuating an ultimately evolving society. Oversimplified, this is why commemorations and observances exist to begin with—immortalizing past triumphs paves the way to repeating the provenly successful, while immortalizing past fallacies forces acknowledgement of shameful blunders and (hopefully) prevents repetition of said blunders. That is, the United States celebrates Black History Month each February and publicly condemns its past institution of slavery. Following World War II, Germany declared November 11th a day of national mourning for all victims, and today, so much as faintly uttering denial of the holocaust is punishable by up to five years in prison. Last spring, while lamenting the Dirty War, during which tens of thousands of dissidents were executed in the late 1970s (much like the 1988 Iranian regime), current Argentinian president Mauricio Macri exclaimed, "Never again in Argentina to political violence, never again to institutional violence."

And so it goes—regimes commit appalling crimes and unimaginable injustices, but eventually, conditions improve, justice is restored, apologies are issued, "days of remembrance" are instituted, and the perpetrators are held to account.

In the Iranian regime's case, however, there is a glaring exception to the aforementioned cycle of events—it never happened. Crimes against humanity did not lose momentum in the years and decades following 1988; in fact, they flourished. The regime never recoiled in shame, never issued a public statement, never so much as implied a formal investigation might be conducted. Like an untreated cancer, the regime's grip on its citizens' liberties metastasized quickly, rapidly snowballing into an avalanche of discourse, violence, and corruption that defines Iran today. Public executions for men, women, and juveniles; unprecedented arrests and detentions; torture of detainees with cables; limb amputation; eye gouging, death sentences for ordinary offenders, political opponents, and blasphemers—these are but a few of the brushstrokes that paint today's Iran.

Inaction and time will never miraculously result in progress. The Iranian regime's current climate proves this without a shadow of a doubt. Since current president, Hassan Rouhani, took office in 2013, it is reported that 3,111 executions (as of September 2017) have occurred on his watch. And it goes without saying, of course, in the country that distinguishes itself as titleholder of most executions per capita on earth, the quality of Iranians' executions is about as inhumane as the quality of their day-to-day lives. The 3,000+ victims executed in these four short years, in many instances in public hangings from cranes, cover a vast demographic –from impoverished substance abusers to persons who were minors at the time of their sentencing to mentally challenged "offenders" to dissidents as well as ethnic and religious minorities. There is no end and there are no exceptions.

The regime's mortifying lag in basic human rights relative to other nations continues without end. While the United States made strides on the global stage with the Civil Rights Movement in the 1960s, and South Africa with its abolishment of apartheid in the 1990s, it has been four decades since the 1979 Revolution, and civil rights in Iran are as nonexistent today as they were then. When it comes to human rights and personal freedoms, for nearly 80 million Iranians, every day is 1988. In this capacity, time has stood still for decades; citizens' rights today are equivalent, if not worse than, the rights of those murdered that fateful summer nearly 30 years ago.

So, again, while this book, and the statements, reports, and accounts that follow herein, center heavily around the 1988 deaths of more than 30,000 prisoners, the purpose of these accounts is not to commemorate the past, but to draw attention to the present as well as the future. Every day, new blood from a new Iranian citizen is spilled at the hands of an inhumane, corrupt, and fear-mongering regime. These figurative hands, however, are the same hands today, as they were thirty years ago.

The 1988 politicide

Twenty-nine years ago, in the summer of 1988, Iranian regime's Supreme Leader, Ayatollah Ruhollah Khomeini, issued a *fatwa* (religious decree) proclaiming, nationwide, any prisoner of conscience in custody who had neither "repented" nor proved willing to cooperate with the regime, would be executed. Based on eyewitness accounts, revelations from the victims' friends and families, and survivors' testimonies, the execution count in that summer alone exceeded 30,000.

Thereafter, the fundamentalist Iranian dictatorship used every suppressive tool and trick in its power to completely conceal the breadth and brutality of the massacre. Information was withheld from both domestic and international media, meaning coverage of the executions was essentially nonexistent. Further, the regime refrained from sending corpses back to their families, as funeral ceremonies would surely serve as incriminating confirmations that the murders had indeed occurred. In fact, the regime was so paranoid over possible exposure of the genocide that Khomeini put his then-successor, Ayatollah Hossein Ali Montazeri, under house arrest when Montazeri vocalized opposition against the carnage. For these reasons, primarily, this story remained untold for many, many years.

For nearly three decades, the People's Mojahedin Organization of Iran (MEK/PMOI), whose activists formed the majority of the victims, and the National Council of Resistance of Iran (NCRI), sought to expose these atrocities to any media outlet or political player willing to listen. But the world's leaders, more transfixed with securing lucrative business and appeasing the regime, rather than prosecuting it, lacked the political will to demand justice.

The deafening silence was shattered on August 9, 2016, however, when an audiotape of Khomeini's successor, Montazeri, was publicized by his son, Ahmad. In the tape, Montazeri is heard berating officials—as it happens, the same regime officials in power today—for their wrongdoings. Montazeri goes on to explain the circumstances that led to the *fatwa*, and expresses his horror over the executions. "The greatest crime committed under the Islamic Republic, from the beginning of the Revolution until now, is this crime committed by you …. members of the judicial system," Montazeri howls.

Montazeri's expressions of horror and repugnance, of course, were neither able to undo the crimes nor bring down justice on the murderous regime. Today is different, though. Today is a new day, and today's readers and audience are more equipped and capable than ever to facilitate justice and awareness for those slain decades ago, at the hands of a regime whose leaders and chiefs still rule unscathed today. This is a book for human rights activists, to raise their voices and demand that the perpetrators are finally held accountable. This is a book for policy-makers, to realize the unethical and shameful nature of keeping silent and making deals with a regime guilty of crimes against humanity. Most importantly, this is a book for anyone and everyone who can find it in his or her conscience to care; for them to acknowledge that the longer they turn a blind eye, the more stained their own hands become, with the blood of Iranians and the blood of those all around the world, who are abused and murdered in the name of power and corruption, every day, and every night.

The killing of even one vulnerable political prisoner is unjustifiable. If the world community is serious about ending the vicious abuses of human rights in Iran, it must take effective steps to end the impunity regarding the 1988 massacre, and halt the unequaled rate of executions. If the world had not kept silent 29 years ago, regard for human rights would be very different in Iran today. And if this silence is broken, the repercussions will be soon and salient.

CHAPTER 1
What Happened

> ❝ The Revolutionary Guards read out about 30
> names, including some of my cellmates. All 30 were
> blindfolded and taken to another part of the hall,
> then led through a door. We later saw the prison
> personnel coming back with wheelbarrows containing
> blindfolds and sandals. All those taken away had been
> executed. Then, some more names were called. ❞
> —**Azadali Hajiloee**, *arrested 1984, imprisoned for 6 years*

In the summer of 1988, "Ayatollah" Ruhollah Khomeini, the founder of the religious dictatorship ruling Iran, issued a hand-written *fatwa* (religious decree), ordering the massacre of political prisoners, a true crime against humanity.[3] The grounds needed to carry out the atrocity had been prepared years before. The mass executions of political prisoners across the country began in the final days of July 1988, and in a matter of months, some 30,000 dissidents, some as young as 14 or 15 at the time of their arrest, were massacred and secretly buried in mass graves.[4]

The massacre was primarily intended, as specified in Khomeini's *fatwa*, to annihilate prisoners supporting the People's Mojahedin Organization of Iran (PMOI/MEK), the core group of the national opposition movement against Khomeini's theocratic regime. Amnesty International stated in a report after the carnage that the massacre of political prisoners was a premeditated and coordinated policy, which had to have been authorized at the highest level of government.[5]

Before the massacre was launched, all family visits with the prisoners were banned. "Death committees" were formed in more than 70 towns and cities, comprised of the most zealous members of the Ministry of Intelligence and Security (MOIS), the judiciary, prosecutors and prison wardens. The plan had been under consideration for years, and its preparations began in the summer of 1988.

Based on eyewitness accounts, the death committees issued their verdicts in sham trials lasting only minutes. There was only one criterion: how would the prisoners refer to their organizational identity? Would they identify as "Mojahedin," (MEK) or *"Monafeqin"* (hypocrites), the derogatory term used by the mullahs?

3   "Deadly *Fatwa*: Iran's 1988 Prison Massacre," *Iran Human Rights Documentation Center*, 15 November 2017, http://www.iranhrdc.org/english/publications/reports/3158-deadly-fatwa-iran-s-1988-prison-massacre.html.

4   Christina Lamb, "Khomeini *fatwa* 'led to killing of 30,000 in Iran'," *The Telegraph*, 4 February 2001, http://www.telegraph.co.uk/news/worldnews/middleeast/iran/1321090/Khomeini-fatwa-led-to-killing-of-30000-in-Iran.html.

5   "Iran still seeks to erase the '1988 prison massacre' from memories, 25 years on," *Amnesty International*, 29 August 2013, https://www.amnesty.org/en/latest/news/2013/08/iran-still-seeks-erase-prison-massacre-memories-years/.

"What is your political affiliation?" government officials would ask.[6] Those who said "Mojahedin" would be told to leave; their names would be placed in the "execution" column, and the sentence would be carried out within hours or days.

Those who said *Monafeqin* would face further questions:

- "Are you prepared to expose and condemn the *Monafeqin* in a televised interview?"

- "Are you prepared to fight the *Monafeqin* alongside the forces of the Islamic Republic?"

- "Are you prepared to put the noose around the neck of an active member of the *Monafeqin*?"

- "Are you prepared to clear minefields for the army of the Islamic Republic?"

A negative answer to any one of these questions would be sufficient to guarantee the execution of the prisoner.

Tehran's prisons, such as Evin and Gohardasht, were the epicenters of the killings, but the death committees visited all prisons across the country to categorize each prisoner.[7] During the weeks that the massacre was in process, all Revolutionary Guards and prison officials were on alert. All leaves were cancelled and the death committees only had access to one telephone line.[8] There were no other forms of communication. Prison staff and wardens were ordered to participate in the executions and to beat the victims after they were hanged. Thus, no one in the system could distance himself far enough to allow him to reveal the atrocity later. This was a successful tactic to keep blood on everyone's hands.

Only very few prisoners who had directly witnessed the executions survived and later escaped.[9] Some had lost their psychological balance and were not able to talk for months after their escapes. Further, only a limited

---

6   National Council of Resistance of Iran, *Crimes Against Humanity* (France, Foreign Affairs Committee of the National Council of Resistance of Iran, 2001), 89.

7   Ibid., 60.

8   Ibid., 89.

9   Ibid., 31.

number of eyewitnesses could flee Iran and testify in front of international sources.

The number of victims was so high that their transportation got out of the regime's control. In one case, while bodies were being transported to mass graves near Ali Abad in the city of Qom, the body of a female victim fell from the truck in front of passersby. The Revolutionary Guards arrested some of the witnesses, or threatened others against revealing what they had seen to anyone.

The MEK and NCRI were able to collect a certain amount of information from their intelligence networks within the country, and from reports of the survivors. However, this was a very dangerous task. A number of prisoners and supporters affiliated with the MEK lost their lives while engaging in collection of the information and photos.[10]

A partial list of the victims includes the identities of 789 minors and 62 pregnant women.[11] It also lists 410 families from which three or more members were executed. This, of course, is only a fraction of the full list of the executed, which the resistance was able to collect under the climate of absolute suppression.

Roghieh Akbari Monfared executed in 1988   Abdolreza Akbari Monfared executed in 1988   Farhad and Farrokh Jareh murdered in 1988

10 Ibid., 117, 128.

11 "62 pregnant women and 789 minors amongst the executed in the mass execution of 1988 in Iran," *International Liberty Association*, 9 September 2016, goo.gl/GCJvqo.

The political prisoners came from all walks of life, reflecting the diversity of public support for the opposition. Most were university students, high school students, or other youth.[12] They were comprised of laborers, farmers, civil employees, doctors and medical professionals, military officers, technical experts, industrial workers, teachers, and professors.[13] Not to mention athletes and artists. The rampage of killings overran every town and city across the country. In some cities, not even a single prisoner survived to tell their story.

Forouzan Abdi, captain of Iran's National Volleyball Team executed in 1988

Mostafa and Khadijeh Mirzaee and Mahnaz Youseffi (left) executed in 1988

Javad Nassiri (first from left), member of Iran's fencing team, executed in 1989

12 National Council of Resistance of Iran, *Crimes Against Humanity* (France, Foreign Affairs Committee of the National Council of Resistance of Iran, 2001), 134.

13 Ibid., 135.

A report from the city of Shiraz is telling: "When word of the killings reached the families of the prisoners, we approached the prison. The henchmen told us, 'Do you expect us to give you sweets? We killed 860 prisoners in one place in one day. And if you hold a funeral, we will destroy your houses with bulldozers.'"

In Isfahan, there was talk of 2,000 executed. In the province of Gilan, word spread that about 3,000 had already been killed.

A crime against humanity was underway, unprecedented since World War II. The question, of course, is how could the world not have known? Why was it so easy for the regime to carry out the secrecy they intended for the death of 30,000 innocent people? What could the world have done then, and what can be done now?

CHAPTER 2
A Survivor's Account

> " ... in an instant, human beings that had overflowed
> from the cells days before, had evaporated,
> all executed in the blink of an eye. "
> —Mostafa Naderi

My story should alarm, should appall. It is a story that should repulse the reader, appear almost implausible that I'm telling the truth. Sadly, my tale is nearly identical to that of thousands of other Iranian youths, pulled from the carnage and chaos that defined the 1980's in Iran.

I was a child when my life changed forever. I couldn't have known what that day in November 1981, in Shemiran cross section, north Tehran, entailed for my future. I couldn't have known I wouldn't be finishing my senior year of high school, that at the ripe age of 17 my life would be hijacked for the next 11 years, teetering between death and torture for more than a decade, before I'd eventually –barely –see the light of day again in 1991.

Like most 17-year-old kids, I was full of curiosity, energy, and passion. Fresh after experiencing an earthshattering revolution, I got engaged in distributing publications and magazines for the Iranian opposition group, the People's Mojahedin Organization of Iran (PMOI), or Mujahedin-e Khalq, (MEK). After all, those were the times of change.

Revolutionary, enlightened ideas and schools of thought raged back and forth all over Iran. The millions who had risked their lives to bring down the Shah's corrupt dictatorship were jubilant; the dark days of despotism had come to an end, and they had high hopes for a democratic, prosperous future. Freedom would reign supreme. The possibilities were endless; nobody knew what the future held. But those beautiful days were short-lived, and those hopes were quickly shattered. The dark clouds of tyranny, this time under the veneer of religion, began to emerge.

I was arrested, along with hundreds if not thousands of others. Suspected of being an MEK supporter, it was expected. The Iranian regime, at this point, was terrified of the MEK and its throngs of supporters and intellectuals overtaking Iran. If an agent had even the slightest hunch that he had encountered an MEK affiliate, like myself, arrest was imminent. The police went after anyone who so much as "looked" intellectual; the youngsters who wore glasses, or those with books in their hands.

I was taken to Evin Prison, the most infamous prison as far as the Iranian regime's crimes against humanity in the 1980s were concerned. My torture commenced almost immediately. I was first taken to a single room already crammed with 500 people. My first nights, anywhere from 150 to 200 prisoners a night were taken away and executed. As fast as prisoners were executed, new arrivals from fresh arrests were spilling into their spaces. Along with hundreds of other terrified detainees, I struggled to stay afloat in the ebb and flow of faces and bodies never to be seen again. During those nights of rapid-fire executions, one could only hope news of his or her execution was printed in the newspapers. This was the only way loved ones would know their beloved had been killed. Thousands and thousands of victims, though, were not lucky enough to have any announcement whatsoever regarding their death. Those families, of course, to this day live without closure.

After eight months at Evin, I was transferred to a different prison in Karaj, west of Tehran, Ghezel Hesar. After a while in Ghezel Hesar, I was taken to a small place called "Gavdooni" (or a place to keep cows), with 65 other cellmates. Each day, once a day, we were fed a spoonful of rice and a piece of bread. In the two and half months I was confined there, I lost nearly 40 pounds, my frame whittling down to nothing more than skin and bones.

Food was the least of the prisoners' worries, though. Many of my cellmates, falling unconscious, tried to be transferred to the infirmary, insisting they were in dire need of aid. Their pleas were met with harsh beatings, further demoralizing them and destroying what remained of their will.

Subsequently, I was transferred to Gohardasht Prison in Karaj, where I spent the next three-year phase of my 11 years in the prison system in solitary confinement. In solitary, I was stripped of all access to, and knowledge of, the outside world. I had no insight into news or current events. I was given neither books nor any materials that would have occupied my mind. I was essentially killed off, without dying.

But I did not die. I was transferred back to Evin Prison, where the torture began again, but this time I was also put into solitary for two more years. At this point, it had been about six years. The year was 1988 and my body was starting to succumb to the years of torture, floggings, lashings with cables on the soles of my feet. I experienced kidney failure due to severe bleeding and lost consciousness. A short time later, I woke up in the hospital prison. An apolitical bedmate asked my name. "They came and called your name several times," he told me. I had no idea what to make of that news, until days later, when I was escorted back to my prison ward, which had been over packed before I fell unconscious, but was now startlingly empty. By word of mouth I learned of Ayatollah Khomeini's *fatwa*, declaring execution for all political prisoners across Iran.

Just like that; in an instant, human beings that had overflowed from the cells days before, had evaporated, all executed in the blink of an eye. Had I not fallen deathly ill, I would have been among the dead.

When it was all said and done, of the 10,000 to 12,000 political prisoners Evin housed, as well as the remaining prisoners in Gohardasht prison which were gathered in Evin, a mere 250 remained; they had lived to tell the tale.

Miraculously, I was released in 1992. Not surprisingly, I spent only a handful of months in Iran before fleeing to Turkey, and then making my way to Canada.

Now troubles of a different kind began. The mass murder of innocents I had witnessed over the course of roughly a decade was a scarring experience I urgently needed to relay to authorities. Yet while I scrambled and scrounged to publish my story in journals and media willing to listen, key political players of the international community were not intrigued. I, and many others who had been lucky enough to escape Iran, were sorely disappointed to realize the political players were downright apathetic. Business with the murderous tyrants was too lucrative to jeopardize by speaking out about the massacre of tens of thousands of defenseless prisoners of conscience, sentenced to death by kangaroo courts. Money was worth more than human lives.

Sadly, this has proven to be a quality of regimes and politicians all over the world, even in our modern battles against inhumanity. Not so much as a slap on the wrist for the Iranian regime. International and human rights organizations issued only apolitical comments along the lines of what had occurred in Iran was unfortunate and a violation of human rights.

After surviving 11 years of isolation and hopelessness, after meeting countless people who I knew suffered death in the most excruciating ways and wouldn't have so much as a tombstone to mark their time on earth, after having cables lashed to the soles of my feet so profusely I was sure at times I'd never walk again. After all of this, I emerged, only to discover I was a pawn in politicians' business transactions and appeasement schemes. That realization should have crushed me. It should have demoralized me beyond words. That realization in itself should have killed me. It didn't. It compelled me to fight harder, yell louder, push back with more might, to work that much more ferociously to make sure you know my story.

My fight for awareness of not just my story, but my friends' and fellow prisoners' stories, has not ceased. I was the lucky one. I am more obligated than ever to tell my story, and theirs; to become the voice of the many thousands who did not survive the horror of 1988. There is still time, there are still world leaders who can make a difference, and there are still readers, like those of this book, who can help magnify the awareness needed for leaders to respond and rectify, even if it's been thirty years. Eleven years in prison did not stop me, neither will thirty. It should not stop you.

Mostafa Naderi

November 2017

CHAPTER 3
Damning Evidence

❝Fifty years from now, they may judge us and say that the Imam was a bloodthirsty killer. We have shown the ugly face of the Supreme Leader. God knows that, as far as the people are concerned, with this extremism and these arrests, we have done this to Islam.❞

—Hossein-Ali Montazeri,
Khomeini's designated successor at the time, August 15, 1988

The Nature of the Crime: Khomeini's *Fatwa*

Unlike most crimes against humanity, there is no ambiguity about the nature or intent of the perpetrators of the 1988 massacre. Their plans were not whispered, their violence not masked. The Supreme Leader of the theocratic regime, "Ayatollah" Ruhollah Khomeini, issued a handwritten decree on or about July 25, 1988[14]:

"As the treacherous *Monafeqin* [*Hypocrites*, a derogatory term used by the regime referring to the MEK] do not believe in Islam and their statements are rooted in deception and hypocrisy, and as their leaders have confessed that they have become renegades, and as they are waging war on God, and as they are engaging in classical warfare on the western, northern and southern fronts, and as they are collaborating with the Baathist Party of Iraq and spying for Saddam [Hussein] against our Muslim nation, and as they are tied to the World Arrogance, and in light of their cowardly blows to the Islamic Republic since its inception, it is decreed that those who are in prison throughout the country and remain steadfast in their support for the *Hypocrites* are waging war on God and are condemned to execution.

"The task of implementing the decree in Tehran is entrusted to Hojja-tol-Islam Nayyeri, the *sharia* [religious] judge; Mr. Eshraqi, the Tehran prosecutor; and a representative of the Intelligence Ministry ...

"In prisons in the provinces, the views of a majority of a trio consisting of the *sharia* judge, the revolutionary prosecutor, and the Intelligence Ministry representative must be obeyed. It is naive to show mercy to those who wage war on God ... Those who are making the decisions must not hesitate, nor show any doubt or be concerned with details..."

Subsequently, Moussavi Ardebili, then Chief Justice, asked Khomeini if the decree applied to those who had been in prison, who had already been tried and sentenced to limited jail terms and who had already served part or all of their terms.

---

14 National Council of Resistance of Iran, Foreign Affairs Committee, *Crime Against Humanity*, 2001, https://www.scribd.com/document/2469298/Crime-Against-Humanity

Khomeini's July 1988 fatwa for the massacre of MEK political prisoners

He also asked: "In reviewing the status of the *Hypocrite* prisoners, is it necessary to refer the cases of *Hypocrite* prisoners in provinces that have an independent judicial organ to the provincial center, or can the province's judicial authorities act autonomously?"

Khomeini's reply removed all doubts, laying bare his evil intention of massacring all political prisoners in Iran's prisons:

"In all the above cases, if the person at any stage or at any time maintains his [or her] support for the *Hypocrites*, the sentence is execution. Annihilate the enemies of Islam immediately. As regards to the cases, use whichever criterion that speeds up the implementation of the verdict."

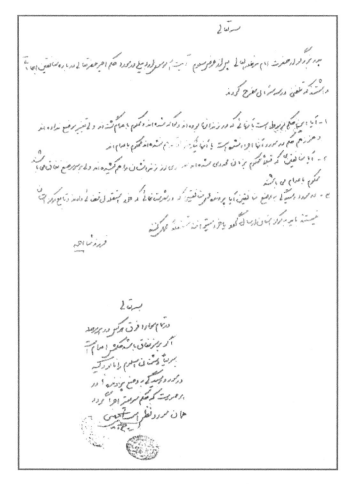

Letter of
Ardabili to
Khomeini
and his
response
clearing
all doubts
for the
massacre

An Atrocity Unparalleled Since WWII:
The Heir Apparent Speaks Out

Among the most telling documents released to the international community by the Iranian opposition were the series of letters recalled in the
memoirs of Ayatollah Montazeri, who had been officially designated as successor to Khomeini at the time.[15] Montazeri objected to Khomeini's decree,
condemning the executions, which he viewed as against the interests of the

15 Ibid.

regime. The execution of several thousand prisoners in a few days would not have positive repercussions, he warned, adding that the Mojahedin were "an idea" and "a logic," which would be strengthened by these killings.

"If you insist on your decree ... spare the women with children," he implored.[16] Khomeini not only ignored his recommendations, but became enraged and ousted Montazeri, who was placed under house arrest until his death in December 2009.[17]

Montazeri wrote two letters to Khomeini and one to officials responsible for implementing the task (members of the death committee in Tehran) in July and August 1988. His first reference to the number of

Ayatollah Hossein-Ali Montazeri was sacked by Khomeini for protesting the 1988 massacre

executed prisoners in the first letter he wrote to Khomeini, dated July 31, 1988, covered only the first days of the massacre when he was still unaware of the mass executions in the provinces; the figures he gave refer only to Tehran. He wrote: "Finally, they executed 2,800 or 3,800 women and men," adding "I doubt either figure is correct."[18]

"The execution of several thousand prisoners in a few days will not have positive repercussions and will not be mistake-free."

"... a judge from Khuzestan by the name of Hojjatol-Islam Mohammad Hossein Ahmadi came to see me and was very distressed. He told me: 'Over there, they are executing them at great speed. They conjure up a majority vote out of the three-member panel. They are angry about the *Monafeqin's* operation, but are venting our anger on the prisoners.'"

16 Ibid.

17 "Grand Ayatollah Hossein Ali Montazeri", *The Telegraph*, 20 December 2009, https://goo.gl/y8nzRq

18 National Council of Resistance of Iran, Foreign Affairs Committee, *Crime Against Humanity*, 2001, https://www.scribd.com/document/2469298/Crime-Against-Humanity

Montazeri's second letter to Khomeini, in which he again protested against the procedure, is dated August 2, 1988.[19] According to his memoirs, he "noticed that they were still continuing the executions. On the first of Moharram, I summoned Mr. Nayyeri, the religious judge of Evin, and Mr. Eshraqi, the prosecutor, and Mr. Raissi, the deputy prosecutor, and Mr. Pour-Mohammadi, the Intelligence Ministry representative. I said to them: 'Now is the month of Moharram and at least halt the executions during this month.'"

In other words, on the first day of the month of Moharram, which coincided with August 13, 1988, mass executions were continuing with the same intensity.

Khomeini issued a second *fatwa* dealing with non-MEK prisoners on September 6 or thereabouts. In Montazeri's words, "they obtained a letter from the Imam [Khomeini] for non-religious [non-Muslim] prisoners.[20] At the time, there were about 500 nonreligious and atheist prisoners. The aim was to liquidate these prisoners, as well, and get rid of them."

By the time this new *fatwa* was issued, mass execution of MEK political prisoners had been going on with ferocity for more than 40 days.

In his memorandum to the members of the "death committee" in Tehran on August 15, 1988, Montazeri referred to the execution of "prisoners and former prisoners," referring to the fact that once the massacre of political prisoners got underway, the clerical regime launched a nationwide effort to re-arrest former political prisoners, in line with Khomeini's *fatwa* that all MEK supporters and members must be executed.[21]

The Coverup: Atrocities Concealed Under a Veil of Silence

Despite Montazeri's objections, and constant efforts by the MEK and NCRI to call international attention to the massacre, for many years the crime against humanity was met with resounding silence. Various

19 Ibid.
20 Ibid.
21 Ibid.

governments cast a blind eye on the bloodbath, with an eye to pursuing their appeasement policy and economic engagement with the regime, dozens of whose current officials were deeply involved in the bloody slaughter. For its part, the regime cast a shadow on the executed by presenting the victims as villains, with conspiracies and allegations of terrorism, etc. adopted by all too willing governments and interlocuters.

Over the years, however, the Iranian Resistance kept up its efforts, word of the genocide did leak, and was reflected by some human rights groups and the media.

Western Media Begin to Address the Massacre

One of the first Western commentators to discuss the killings in Iran was Christina Lamb, the Diplomatic Correspondent for the Telegraph. Her article, published in February of 2001, describes the events in Iran in detail. She chronicles the murder of "children as young as 13" hanging from cranes as punishment for their political opposition. Her information comes from the memoirs of Grand Ayatollah Hossein-Ali Montazeri, one of the founders of the Islamic regime. The 'death committees' are also mentioned in her work as she describes their role in the killing of the 30,000. Lamb recalls the letters and documents published, including "Khomeini's fatwa decree calling for all Mojahedin (as opponents of the Iranian regime are known) to be killed" and describes the letters as "the most damning" evidence.

Her coverage of the 1988 massacre brought the harsh realities of the regime's past actions into the public's attention. She even goes as far to directly call out members of the current regime for their past actions stating that "many of those in the ruling council at the time of the 1988 massacre are still in power, including President Mohammed Khatami, who was the Director of Ideological and Cultural Affairs." She highlights the lack of action by the United Nations, "no action was taken by the UN or any other international body to hold the ruling regime accountable and bring the perpetrators to justice."[22]

(See the Appendix for Mr. Montazeri's three letters to Khomeini and the 'death committee" members)

The Black Box: A Massacre Exposed

On August 9, 2016, twenty-eight years after the carnage, the audio recording of Montazeri's meeting (referred to above) with those responsible for the massacre of MEK political prisoners was published on Montazeri's official website by his son, Ahmad Montazeri.[23] Ahmad Montazeri has since been sentenced to 21 years in prison.

A report of the UN Secretary General, Antonio Guterres, on the situation of human rights in Iran in March 2017 reads: "The trial of Mr. Montazeri was reportedly held behind closed doors, and he was prevented from choosing his own lawyer. The Secretary-General's predecessor expressed deep concern over the imprisonment of Mr. Montazeri and the apparent lack of investigation into the revelations contained in the audio recording."[24]

The audio file was a recording of a meeting held on August 15, 1988, with the so called "Death Committee" consisting of four people: Mostafa Pour Mohammadi, representative of the Ministry of Intelligence (MOIS) in Evin Prison; Hossein Ali Nayyeri, Sharia judge; Morteza Eshraghi, public prosecutor; and Ebrahim Raisi, deputy prosecutor, who collectively decided on the executions in Tehran. Similar committees were formed in the provinces and other cities.

The tape blew the lid off the coverup imposed by the regime for almost three decades, and exposed the fundamental involvement of both

22 Christina Lamb. "Khomeini *fatwa* 'led to killing of 30,000 in Iran", *The Telegraph*, 04 February 2001, https://goo.gl/mMRDTC

23 Audiotape of 1988 Conversation of Ayatollah Montazeri with the "Death Committee" members revealed in August 2016, BBC Persian, https://soundcloud.com/bbcpersian/1367a

24 Secretary General of the Human Rights Council, "Situation of human rights in the Islamic Republic of Iran". *United Nations Human Rights Council*, 13 March 2017, https://goo.gl/UcntAu

the "hardline" faction of current Supreme Leader Ali Khamenei and the "moderate" faction of current President Hassan Rouhani, then deputy to former President and "king-maker" Ali-Akbar Hashemi Rafsanjani.

Excerpts of the tape:

Montazeri: *"In the (prisons) in cities they did everything imaginable ... in Ahvaz, it was truly awful."*

A member of the Death Committee: *"Many of those on death row have other members of their family who were executed, some were 15-16 years old at the time of their arrest."*

Montazeri: *"This judge or that judge, in this town or in that town, had condemned someone to 5, 6, 10 or 15 year sentences. Well, now if we go and execute them without any new activity, that means our entire judicial system is flawed."*

Montazeri: *"Three days ago the Sharia judge of one of the provinces, who is a trustworthy man, came to me with sadness and said the intelligence official or the prosecutor, in order to determine if a prisoner was steadfast or not, asked him 'Are you ready to condemn the Hypocrites?' He said, 'yes.' He was asked, 'Are you ready to give an interview?' He said, 'yes.' Asked, 'Are you ready to go to war with Iraq?' He said, 'yes.' Asked, 'Are you ready to go on the minefield?' He said, 'not all people are ready to go on a mine.' The judge said, 'Then you are steadfast,' and they executed him."*

Montazeri: *"This one guy, his brother was in prison... They said his sister was also a suspect. So they went and brought his sister. They executed him. They had brought his sister only two days earlier; they questioned her, she said well I liked these people [MEK]. She was only 15 or 16 years old... she is only a girl. He [the judge] replied: execute her too, and they did."*

Montazeri: *"In Isfahan a pregnant woman was among them (the victims); in Isfahan they executed a pregnant woman."*

Montazeri: *"In Shiite Jurisprudence, women should not be executed even if she is 'Mohareb' (at war with God), I reminded Khomeini that according to the decrees of most religious experts, a woman, even if she is a Mohareb must not be executed. But he did not agree, and said that women, too, must be executed."*

Montazeri: *"I said to Ahmad Agha [Khomeini's son], I feel heartbroken for Khomeini. I did not want it to be like this. People are disgusted by the velayat-e-faqih (absolute rule of supreme clergy). I did not want the velayat-e-faqih to come to this point. … Fifty years from now, they may judge us and say that the Imam was a bloodthirsty killer. We have shown the ugly face of the Supreme Leader. God knows that, as far as the people are concerned, with this extremism and these arrests, we have done this to Islam.* ”[25]

The Numbers: How Many?

For years after the 1988 massacre, no one could confirm how many people had been executed. The pattern of political executions had changed dramatically, and international human rights advocates went from piecemeal reports of executions to accounts of a massive wave of killings which took place over several months. By the time the carnage came to a halt, the Iranian authorities were scrambling to prevent word getting out about the scope of the massacre.

The MEK started collecting information as early as August 1988, immediately after learning that mass killings were taking place in the prisons, and issued statements in an attempt to convey the magnitude of the atrocity, although the names and details of all the victims were not accessible.

Amnesty International recorded the names of over 2,000 political prisoners reportedly executed during this period.[26] Amnesty interviewed family members and survivors who dared to speak, of course anonymously. These accounts, taken together with statements by Iranian government personalities, convinced Amnesty International that during a six-month period, the biggest wave of political executions since the early 1980s had taken place in Iranian prisons.

Reynaldo Galindo Pohl, the Special Rapporteur of the Commission of Human Rights on Iran, reported the carnage to the Human Rights Commission, listing the names of over 1,000 victims.[27]

25 Audiotape of 1988 Conversation of Ayatollah Montazeri with the "Death Committee" members revealed in August 2016, https://soundcloud.com/bbcpersian/1367a

26 IRAN: VIOLATIONS OF HUMAN RIGHTS 1987 - 1990", *Amnesty International*, 1 December 1990, https://goo.gl/DhzcrJ

27 Reynaldo Galindo Pohl, "Question of the Violation of Human Rights and Fundamental Freedoms in any Part of the World, with Particular Reference to Colonial and Other Dependent Countries and Territories," *United Nations Commission on Human Rights*, 16 January 1995, https://goo.gl/GUH5yC

Three brothers Ardekan, Ardeshir, and Ardalan Darafarin executed, two in 1988 massacre

The question remained, how many?

Mr. Kamal Afkhami Ardekani, a former official at Evin prison, has said in testimonies to human rights rapporteurs of the United Nations: "In July 1988, after Khomeini issued a *fatwa* ordering the massacre of Mojahedin prisoners, a meeting was held in Evin prison... There they agreed on the procedures for carrying out Khomeini's orders. They would line up prisoners in a 14-by-5-meter hall in the central office building of Evin. The maximum capacity of the hall was 180 prisoners. They would then ask simply one question: 'What is your political affiliation?' Those who said the Mojahedin, would be hanged from cranes that had been in position behind the building."[28]

28 Christina Lamb, *Khomeini fatwa 'led to killing of 30,000 in Iran'*, Daily Telegraph, Feb. 4, 2001, available at http://www.telegraph.co.uk/news/worldnews/middleeast/iran/1321090/Khomeini-fatwa-led-to-killing-of-30000-in-Iran.html

Shekar Mohammadzadeh, a nurse, executed in 1988

Monireh Rajavi, murdered in 1988 for being the sister of the Iranian resistance leader Massoud Rajavi

"Prisoners were hanged in Evin prison with six cranes and three fork-lift trucks. Each time, 33 people would be hanged. On each crane, there was an iron beam and five ropes were suspended from the beam. The six cranes were positioned in these locations: one was placed next to the administrative courtroom building, two were placed next to Ward 325, and three were placed next to the special ward for the clergy and the central administrative building.

"The fork-lift trucks, each fitted with a beam with four ropes, were placed in the parking lot outside the prosecutor's office. The parking lot was also used as an execution yard. There was a crane in the garage next to the parking lot and that was also used for executions.

"The mass executions began in late July 1988. Every half an hour, 33 persons were being hanged by these cranes and the process went on and on without any interruption… Once they were pronounced dead, the bodies would be piled into covered trucks and taken out of prison. The trucks had been on loan from Evin's police station. Some of the trucks belonged to Evin prison itself.

"The same procedure went on for two weeks, from 7:30 am until 5 pm. Soon they were also using the parking lot for the executions and the number of executions every half-hour reached 37 to 40," Afkhami Ardekani said.[29]

On the basis of these revelations by a former official of Evin prison, it can be safely extrapolated that if 19 rounds of executions were carried out every day, and in each round 30 prisoners were hanged, then at least 570 prisoners were being executed in Evin prison every day. In 14 days, the number of executions exceeds 8,000. Bearing in mind that executions were continuing even after two weeks, and that by early September Khomeini issued another decree ordering the execution of non-MEK prisoners who, according to Montazeri[30], numbered about 500, then the number of male prisoners executed in Evin prison was more than 10,000. There were thousands of women prisoners, many of whom were executed.

In addition, there were thousands of inmates in other jails in and around Tehran, including Gohardasht, where the massacre was carried out with equal ferocity. When all these are added together, the number of executions in Tehran jails becomes exceedingly high. One must also bear in mind that the Iranian Resistance had revealed a list of 635 prisons with addresses and their specifications, which gives an idea of the magnitude of the carnage.

Reports compiled by the Iranian opposition show that the carnage went on in at least 100 cities and towns across the country. In many of these cities, not a single political prisoner was left alive. These cities included Kermanshah, Zanjan, Mashhad, Arak, Hamadan, Orumiyeh, Semnan, Roudsar, Ahvaz, Qom, Sari, Qaemshahr, Shahr-e Kord, Khorramabad, Zahedan, Karaj, Tabriz, Sabzevar, Rasht, Shiraz, Masjed- Soleyman, Isfahan, Sanandaj, Babol, Lahijan, Bandar-Anzali, Chalous, Borujerd, Kashan, Manjil, Garmsar, Fasa, Andimeshk, Behbahan, Kalachai, Gachsaran, Kerman, Sowme'e-Sara, Abhar, Shahinshahr, Dezful, Islamabad, Kerend, Ilam, Borazjan, Toyserkan, Pol Dokhtar, Ardabil, Shahroud, Gorgan, Gonabad, Shahreza, Langaroud, Amol, Aligoodarz, Quchan, Maku, Qazvin,

29 National Council of Resistance of Iran, Foreign Affairs Committee, *Crime Against Humanity*, 2001, https://www.scribd.com/document/2469298/Crime-Against-Humanity

30 Ibid.

Birjand, Maragheh, Mahshahr, Bushehr, Khoy, Kazeroun, Salmas, Golpayegan, Estahbanat, Aliabad, and so on.

Amnesty International reported that it was receiving information pointing to hundreds of executions from among the Kurdish opposition group prisoners in the prison of Orumiyeh, and 50 executions in Sanandaj[31]. Throughout the rest of 1988, there were reports on continuing executions in different parts of Iran.

- In Orumiyeh, around 400 prisoners were executed and buried in mountains around the city in groups of 10, 20, and 30 people (November 8, 1988)

- In Semnan, eight prisoners supporting the Mojahedin were hanged in public from a construction crane, (November 8, 1988).

- 18 prisoners in Arak, an unspecified number of prisoners in Rudsar, dozens of prisoners in Ahwaz, 18 prisoners in Astara and another group of prisoners in Shahre-Kord were sent to the firing squad, (November 8, 1988).

- In November 1988, further reports on more executions in different cities began coming in. According to these reports which were confirmed by different sources, 84 people were executed in Mashhad prison in October. Also in October, 150 prisoners were executed in the prison of Khorramabad (western Iran). Twenty-one prisoners were executed in Tabriz prison (December 2, 1988).

Manjil - Following torrential rains, a mass grave containing 80 bodies of political prisoners was discovered two kilometers west of the Tehran-Rasht highway.

Garmsar - Two truckloads of bodies of prisoners were transferred from Evin and Qezel Hessar prisons to wastelands around the city and buried in a big mass grave.

Southwestern Iran - 33 MEK supporters were executed over several weeks in the cities of Ahvaz, Andimeshk and Behbahan. Among them were at least seven women. At the same time, more than 20 political prisoners were executed in Bushehr.

31 "IRAN: VIOLATIONS OF HUMAN RIGHTS 1987-1990," *Amnesty International*

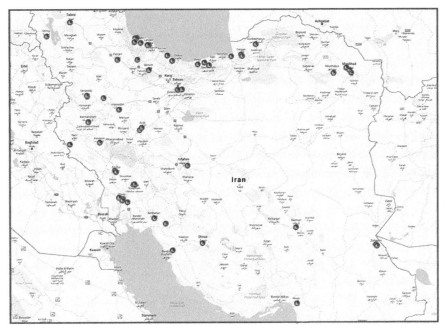

Map of cities where mass graves of 1988 massacre victims have been identified in Iran

Sabzevar - 29 MEK supporters were executed after years of imprisonment.

Southern Iran - 26 political prisoners, who were completing their prison terms, were executed in Fasa. Also in Adelabad prison in Shiraz 14 inmates were executed in one day.

Northern Iran - Following the discovery of 10 corpses belonging to MEK prisoners buried in two mass graves in Kalachai and Roudsar, citizens clashed with the Guards.

Tabriz - Four opponents of the regime were hanged in one of the city's circles. The bodies were left hanging for 24 hours, (January 2, 1989).

All political prisoners in the prisons of Dizelabad (Kermanshah), Vakilabad (Mashhad), Gachsaran, Khorramabad, Kerman and Masjed Soleyman had been executed by January 10, 1989.

The Guards dug a big mass grave near Sowme'e-Sara - Kasma road in the Northern Province of Gilan, and during one night buried several truckloads of corpses in it.

Near Khavaran road (east of Tehran), agents of the Revolutionary Prosecutor's Office buried the bodies of a large group of the executed beside the Armenian cemetery. Stray dogs dug out some corpses from shallow graves, and the mass graves were exposed.

In Isfahan, in the beginning of 1989, bodies of executed political prisoners were buried in groups of 40, 60 and 100 in Bagh-e-Rezvan cemetery.

In Tehran, agents of the regime buried corpses of a large number of massacre victims in a big canal in Behesht-e Zahra Cemetery's Block 93. In blocks no 106, 107, 108 and 109 of the same cemetery; the graves of a considerable number of executed prisoners have been discovered by their families.

Ninety-four people from the town of Abhar, 60 people from Khazaneh (southern Tehran), 40 people from the residents of Ray Street, and 11 people from Norouzkhan district in Tehran's Bazaar were executed (December 31, 1988).

In a suburb of Isfahan called Shahinshahr, 700 people were executed over several months. During the last days of 1988, 10 MEK members were

A mass grave in the city of Ahvaz

Victims of 1988 massacre in a mass grave in Mashhad cemetery

A mass grave in Khavaran cemetery in Tehran

A woman laying a wreath at Khavaran cemetery in Tehran

The victims of 1988 massacre in Khavaran Cemetery in Tehran

A mass grave in Vadi-Rahmat Cemetery in Tabriz

hanged in public in one day in three different places in the city of Islamabad (western Iran), while 40 people were executed by firing squad in the northern city of Lahijan.

Mass executions and public hangings continued at the same rate in towns all over the country. Thirty-one people in Sanandaj, 25 in Borazjan, 27 in Baneh were executed. In only one village named Dehkohneh, in the vicinity of Borazjan, five MEK supporters were sent to the firing squad. In Tagh Nosrat district of Toyserkan, three supporters of MEK were hanged in public in one day. In Karaj, the extent of secret executions of political prisoners was extremely high, leaving only three people from 500 in one ward of Gohardasht prison (February 10, 1988).

The Plot: When, and Why Then?

Two important political events preceded the executions. On July 18, 1988, then Supreme Leader Khomeini announced his intention to accept UN Security Council Resolution 598 instituting a ceasefire in the Persian Gulf War between Iran and Iraq.[32] A few days later, the National Liberation

32 National Council of Resistance of Iran, Foreign Affairs Committee, *Crime Against Humanity*, 2001, https://www.scribd.com/document/2469298/Crime-Against-Humanity

Army, a military force formed by the MEK, staged an armed incursion into western Iran, which was repulsed by the Iranian regime. Some had suggested that one or both of these events might have influenced the government's decision to carry out the executions at that time.

The ceasefire in the Persian Gulf War meant that international attention was focused on international developments, and not on the situation of political prisoners in Iran. Former prisoners have also said that political prisoners were warned by their captors that when the war was over they would be "dealt with."

There is also a narrative that the armed incursion by the MEK, gave the authorities a motive to take reprisals against prisoners associated with the MEK, who had been held in prisons around the country, often for several years.

However, the audio-tape of Montazeri's conversation with members of the "death committee" revealed on August 9, 2016 discloses that no matter how much the above two factors might have accelerated the massacre, the decision had been made years before. Montazeri is heard to say, "This [the mass executions] was planned long ago and is something that Intelligence [Ministry] was planning, and had invested in, and Ahmad Agha [Khomeini's son], has been saying for three or four years that 'The Mojahedin [MEK], from the one who reads their newspaper, to the one who reads their magazine, to the one who reads their statements—all of them must be executed.'"

As some of the victims' families testified later, worrying signs had started coming out of the prisons in Spring 1987. An Iranian refugee residing in Paris by the name of Zohreh Bijanyar, whose sister was a political prisoner slaughtered in the 1988 massacre, testified in one of the sequential "Popular Tribunals" arranged by the NCRI Judicial Commission in 2000: "… In one of my visits to my sister in late March 1988, I was informed by her and other prisoners that all political prisoners were going to be executed. They told us that all political prisoners had been categorized and on many occasions separated from each other. This was something I had heard many times from family members of other prisoners too who had come to visit their relatives in prison."

Reza Shemirani, a survivor of the 1988 massacre arrested in July 1981, stated in his testimony to the Boroumand Foundation: "In the fall of 1987, when I was in Branch 13, my interrogator told me that they had a plan for prisoners, and this plan was being carried out. In return for my cooperation, he said, 'I will send you somewhere where you wouldn't be with your friends and you could save face.'

"He did not tell me what these plans were, but around the same time, in the fall of 1987, they took Masoud Moqbeli [another political prisoner] to the Moshtarak Committee. They made him listen to Radio Mojahed. They told him, 'Go back to your ward and tell the prisoners that we don't want prisoners anymore; that we have categorized prisoners into red, yellow, and white. We will execute those categorized as red and release the whites and will make a decision about the yellows.'

"They also took one of the Tudeh [communist] kids and told him the same thing. In my opinion, the executions of 1988 were not triggered by the attack of the MEK. From a year before, the regime had a plan. It is possible that, at that juncture, they just accelerated the process. There were signs indicating that the regime intended to move toward executions."

CHAPTER 4

Officials Acknowledge a Crime Against Humanity

> " I was told by other prisoners when I got out that in some of the other sections, only a handful survived, meaning well over 90 to 95 percent were executed...My father-in-law was one of those executed during the massacre. They told his family to sign papers to say that he had died in a car crash or of a heart attack as a condition to revealing the whereabouts of his grave. "
>
> —Heidar Yousefli,
> *62, arrested on 7 February 1982. Time spent in prison, 12 years.*

In summer of 1988, more than 30,000 political prisoners in Iran were executed in a matter of a few months. Supreme Leader Ruhollah Khomenei issued a *fatwa* order instructing "death committees" to carry out executions of Mujahedin-e-Khalq (MEK) members and other leftists, giving them "trials" that lasted only minutes.

Any mention of the 1988 massacre was taboo in Iran for almost three decades. Repercussions were severe against families who insisted on answers, and against activists who raised the issue on social media or elsewhere. The authorities never publicly acknowledged the events of 1988. However, the Iranian presidential election of 2017 brought the issue to the forefront when Ebrahim Raisi announced his candidacy, challenging incumbent Hassan Rouhani after his first term.[33] When the audiotaped meeting between Hossein Ali Montazeri and the members of the Tehran "death commission" in 1988 was leaked, mud slinging began to focus on Raisi's history as a member of that commission. This was countered by revelations of the role that Rouhani's choice for his Justice Minister, Mostafa Pour-Mohammadi, had played in that same commission.

Hassan Rouhani came under attack during 2017 presidential elections for ties with 1988 massacre

Several of the perpetrators are currently holding key positions in the Iranian judiciary and government. Members of the "death committees" established in 1988 remain high-ranking officials today, including the current justice minister, Alireza Avayi. Regrettably, there is no sign of remorse on the part of the authorities for what had happened in 1988 and throughout the 1980s.

Alireza Avayi, the new justice minister of Hassan Rouhani, Death Committee member in 1988

33 Fitch, Asa, Hard-Line Cleric Ebrahim Raisi Launches Bid for Iranian Presidency, *Wall Street Journal*, April 9, 2017, https://www.wsj.com/articles/hard-line-cleric-ebrahim-raisi-launches-bid-for-iranian-presidency-1491780106

However, since the summer of 2016, state media has begun covering issues related to Khomeini's *fatwa*. The current public awareness regarding this issue has forced the government to change its strategy, and they now argue that they had implemented the divine will as decreed in the Supreme Leader's *fatwa*.

Along these lines, members of the Iranian government have begun to acknowledge the occurrence of the "summer of blood" over the course of the past two years. A vigorous campaign by the Iranian opposition and youth highlighted the need for this recognition, and advocated providing information to the victims' families. Beginning in 2016, the regime finally started openly acknowledging the massacre.

On August 27, 2016, Supreme Leader Ali Khamenei claimed that "evil hands" are "trying to create an atmosphere of innocence" for the MEK, saying that they "have killed thousands of ordinary people and officials and renowned dignitaries."[34] Khamenei flips the blame onto the victims by asserting that it is they who are the criminals.

Khamenei also came to the defense of Raisi during the presidential campaign as allegations relating him to the 1988 massacre began to surface.[35] In June of 2017, he stated "Recently, there have been some voices and advocates of those voices attacking [the incidents of] the 1980s…The terrorist hypocrites [MEK] and their supporters and the powers that created them and boasted about them treated the people of Iran with cruelty. The people of Iran were in a defensive posture."[36] Once again, Khamenei rationalized the horrific acts of the regime by blaming his opponents and calling them terrorists. In the minds of the regime, the massacre was necessary from a religious standpoint, and the *fatwa* issued by Khomeini was merely an extension of the requirement to stamp out dissenters and "protect" the regime.

Mostafa Pour-Mohammadi, the current Justice Minister who was appointed by the so-called "moderate" president Rouhani, also showed no remorse for the 1988 massacre. Justifying the regime's atrocities, he stated:

34 http://www.leader.ir/fa/content/16135/

35 https://www.washingtonpost.com/news/monkey-cage/wp/2017/04/27/irans-holding-presidential-elections-here-are-the-candidates-to-watch/?utm_term=.447e3cd89056

36 Khamenei's speech on the anniversary of death of Khomeini, June 3, 2017, Khamenei website, http://farsi.khamenei.ir/speech-content?id=36745

"God commanded, show no mercy to the non-believers because they will not show mercy to you; there should be no mercy for the [MEK] because if they could, they would spill your blood, ...We are proud to have carried out God's commandment with regard to the [Mojahedin] and to have stood with strength and fought against the enemies of God and the people."[37] Pour-Mohammadi was also a member of the death committees, and is one of many current officials that bridges the gap between the injustices of the past and present regimes.

Similarly, current Head of the Judiciary Sadeq Larijani said in August 2016 that the MEK and its affiliates are wrongly attempting to sway public opinion. Issuing an implied threat, he stated, "the Judiciary will act forcefully, as always, and any disturbance in public opinion on these security issues will certainly face prosecution by the Judiciary."[38] It is clear that the current rulers have no issue continuing the actions and trends set by the regime during the 1988 massacre, and still strongly believe that political dissidents like the MEK should face severe punishment because of their positions.

The support for the actions of 1988 extends to the Islamic Revolutionary Guard Corps (IRGC) and its affiliates as well, a group established after the 1979 revolution as a branch of Iran's armed forces. Mohammad-Reza Naqdi, head of the IRGC-affiliated Bassij Mostazafan Organization, justified Khomeini's order by saying it was in "full compliance with all judicial, religious, legal, Islamic, international and domestic standards... *Fatwas* issued by Imam [Khomeini] are based on solid religious and judicial foundations."[39] It's worth noting that the IRGC has been subjected to sanctions by the U.S. government, having been designated as a terrorist organization in October 2017.[40]

37 Pour-Mohammadi speech in Khorramabad, *We Are Proud to Have Carried Out God's Command Against Monafeqin [MEK]*, reported by Tasnim News Agency, August 28, 2016, https://www.tasnimnews.com/fa/news/1395/06/07/1170966

38 Reaction of Sadegh Larijani to release of Montazeri tape, *Crimes of Monafeqin Can Not Be Washed*, Fars News Agency, August 15, 2016, http://www.farsnews.com/newstext.php?nn=13950525000961

39 Mohammad Reza Naqdi speech in Mashhad, Execution of Monafeqin in 1988 was completely right, IRNA, August 30, 2016, http://www.irna.ir/fa/News/82210739/

40 Non-proliferation Designations; Iran Designations; Counter Terrorism Designation Update, U.S. Department of the treasury, October 13, 2017, https://www.treasury.gov/resource-center/sanctions/OFAC-Enforcement/Pages/20171013.aspx

Crucially, former minister of the IRGC Mohsen Rafiqdoost backed these claims in 2017, and noted that the regime would have no problem enacting the same policies today. Emphasizing that the MEK posed a threat to the regime's goals, he stated that "If the arrested [MEK] elements were not executed, it was feared that they would make the revolution deviate… Today too, the order remains valid: if we find [MEK members], we will do the same to them."[41] Nothing has changed within the Iranian regime—the orders still stand to execute political dissidents and prosecute citizens simply because of their beliefs.

The Assembly of Experts and its members have also been vocal regarding the 1988 massacre. Its official website praises "the historic and revolutionary decision of His Eminence Imam Khomeini in his decisive and uncompromising action toward the [MEK]" and describes "the deep understanding and foresightedness of that heavenly man in saving the Islamic regime."[42] Ahmad Khatami, a member of the Assembly of Experts, stated that "What the late Imam did in 1988 was a religious, Quranic and revolutionary act, and it was a great service to the Muslim nation of Iran… We owe our security today to the Imam's revolutionary measure."[43] He later claimed, "all the people that complied with his edict should be awarded a medal of honor."[44]

Mehdi Khazali, a former official in the office of the president, actually recognized the number of political prisoners that were killed in the regime's massacre and justified the action. Khazali said that the officials "said that if anyone was released [from prison], he/she would become a renegade; then we would be entangled in a situation where we would be facing many people. So, we should execute these people, and their executions would terrify their families and no one would dare to become a renegade…Nearly 33,000

41 Interview with Mohsen Rafiqdoost, Mehr News Agency, July 18, 2017 http://www.mehrnews.com/news/4032488/

42 Statement issued by the Assembly of Experts, Fars News Agency, August 28, 2016, http://www.farsnews.com/newstext.php?nn=13950607000396

43 Friday Prayers speech by Ahmad Khatami, reported by Kayhan Newspaper, August 19, 2016, http://kayhan.ir/fa/news/83162/795

44 Friday Prayers speech by Ahmad Khatami, July 21, 2017, https://www.youtube.com/watch?v=w68jLrWJ8i4 also see, IRIB, http://www.iribnews.ir/fa/news/1727704/

people were hanged in a matter of a month or so."[45] This recognition is key, because the regime had never before acknowledged exactly how many Iranians had been executed.

Supreme Leader Ali Khamenei, official website, August 24, 2016

"Unfortunately, some people are trying to create an atmosphere of innocence for criminals [the victims] who have killed thousands of ordinary people and officials and renowned dignitaries, and distort the radiant image of the late Imam [Khomeini]. But these evil hands will not succeed and they will fail as they have done before."[46]

Ali-Akbar Hashemi Rafsanjani, former President and Head of the State Expediency Council, state-run Fars News Agency, August 27, 2016

"The wave has embraced virtually all foreign opposition media, to the extent that the Mayor of Paris recently held an exhibition which recreated the scenes of executions in those days. The extent of current support for this terrorist group [MEK] merits consideration. The main objective of our international and domestic enemies is to take revenge from the unprecedented role and status of the Imam [Khomeini] in the contemporary history of Iran and the world. We must act vigilantly and describe the Imam's path in a way that cannot be abused by opponents."[47]

Mostafa Pour-Mohammadi, Justice Minister, August 28, 2016

"God commanded, show no mercy to the non-believers because they will not show mercy to you; there should be no mercy for the [MEK] because if

---

45 Khazali, Mehdi, interview with Dorr TV, August 28, 2016, http://www.dorrnews. com/?p=6261 also see, https://www.youtube.com/watch?v=J0okdDyHDMY

46 Ali Khamenei meeting with president and cabinet members, Khamenei website, August 24, 2016, http://www.leader.ir/fa/content/16135/

47 Hashemi Rafsanjani, Ali Akbar, address to the Expediency Council, August 27, 2016, http://www.farsnews.com/newstext.php?nn=13950606001372

they could, they would spill your blood, ...We are proud to have carried out God's commandment with regard to the [Mojahedin] and to have stood with strength and fought against the enemies of God and the people."[48]

Assembly of Experts, official website, August 28, 2016

"Perhaps, for some, it is still hard to grasp the historic and revolutionary decision of His Eminence Imam Khomeini in his decisive and uncompromising action toward the [MEK] and the prosecution of the leaders and some members of the [MEK] in 1988, and the deep understanding and foresightedness of that heavenly man in saving the Islamic regime, which is the fruit of the struggle and

Mostafa Pourmohammadi, Rouhani's Justice Minister till 2017, member of Death Committee in 1988

efforts of the old and the young in this country. The late Imam arrested the sedition through his timely decision at that critical juncture.

Assembly of Experts in 2016 fully endorsed the 1988 massacre

48 Pour-Mohammadi speech in Khorramabad, *We Are Proud to Have Carried Out God's Command Against Monafeqin [MEK]*, reported by Tasnim News Agency, August 28, 2016, https://www.tasnimnews.com/fa/news/1395/06/07/1170966

"Isn't it the case that the heartless [MEK], whose crimes and treachery against this land are a well-known fact, have from time to time with the various support of the Arrogance [the West] and reactionary states sought to revive their evil and corrupt existence?

"While condemning the crimes of the evil [MEK] grouplet in Iran and Iraq, the Assembly of Experts condemns the publication of this audio tape by the supporters of this grouplet, which only adds fuel to the fire of the enemy, and it warns the wise and aware people, in particular the dear youth of Islamic Iran, that the [MEK], guilty of all those crimes and organizationally fragmented, is on the brink of total destruction and will get nowhere through such hopeless attempts to stain the truth about His Eminence the Imam [Khomeini] and the holy regime of the Islamic Republic of Iran. They will not reduce by an iota the firm belief of you, the wise and pious people, in the path of the Imam and the Revolution."[49]

Ahmad Khatami, Tehran Friday Prayer Leader and Member of the Assembly of Experts, August 19, 2016

"Those who had collaborated in prison and said that we were steadfast, they too are *Mohareb* [at war with God]...What the late Imam did in 1988 was a religious, Quranic and revolutionary act, and it was a great service to the Muslim nation of Iran. If the Imam had not committed that brave act, we would have had big issues today; we wouldn't have had security. We owe our security to-

Ahmad Khatami, Tehran Friday Prayer Leader says 1988 massacre was religious duty

day to the Imam's revolutionary measure...People should not believe whatever is broadcast from foreign satellite networks."[50]

49 Statement issued by the Assembly of Experts, Fars News Agency, August 28, 2016, http://www.farsnews.com/newstext.php?nn=13950607000396

50 Friday Prayers speech by Ahmad Khatami, reported by Kayhan Newspaper, August 19, 2016, http://kayhan.ir/fa/news/83162/795

Mohsen Rafiqdoost, former Minister of the IRGC, August 28, 2016

"The Imam [Khomeini] wrote in his will that he would go to an eternal place with a calm and certain heart because, if he had not resolved the problem of the [MEK], the revolution would have faced problems."[51]

Sadeq Larijani, Head of the Judiciary, August 15, 2016

"Western countries and their regional proxies try to support the [PMOI] by inviting them to Paris and holding rallies, and, unfortunately, some inside the country also try to somehow go along with this movement and disturb public opinion. But they should know that the Judiciary will act forcefully, as always, and any disturbance in public opinion on these security issues will certainly face prosecution by the Judiciary...What has been done based on the verdicts of the courts cannot be compromised, and the verdict for *Mohareb* [enmity against God] groups is very clear, but, unfortunately, some go the crooked way and say strange things."[52]

Ali Razini, President of Branch 41 Supreme Court, August 16, 2016

"Unfortunately, there are strategies active inside and outside the country to somehow revive the MEK... whose verdict was *'moharebeh'* [enmity with God], their sentences were carried out, and the basis for other problems was annihilated. The security that we have now in Iran, which shines as an island of stability among all insecure countries in the region, is because Imam Khomeini did not neglect to carry out the sentence...We are thankful to the Founder of the Islamic Revolution who acted with such decisiveness and prevented the penetration of insecurity."[53]

51 Speech by Mohsen Rafiqdoost, August 28, 2016, Tasnim News agency, https://www.tasnimnews.com/fa/news/1395/06/07/1170993/

52 Reaction of Sadegh Larijani to release of Montazeri tape, *Crimes of Monafeqin Can Not Be Washed*, Fars News Agency, August 15, 2016, http://www.farsnews.com/newstext.php?nn=13950525000961

53 Razini, Ali, interview with Mashregh News, August 16, 2016, http://www.mashreghnews.ir/fa/news/618892/

Mehdi Khazali, former official in the Office of the President, August 26, 2016

"The largest and most popular group which opposed the state was the People's Mojahedin Organization...It could be annihilated only by authorization from the Imam [Khomeini]. In fact, they wanted to uproot this group while the Imam was still alive. They said that if anyone was released [from prison], he/she would become a renegade; then we would be entangled in a situation where we would be facing many people. So, we should execute these people, and their executions would terrify their families and no one would dare to become a renegade...Nearly 33,000 people were hanged in a matter of a month or so."[54]

Mehdi Khazali says 33,000 were massacred in 1988

Ali Khamenei, Iran's Supreme Leader speaking in defense of Ebrahim Raisi, official website, June 3 2017

"Recently, there have been some voices and advocates of those voices attacking [the incidents of] the 1980s. My advice to all those theorists and intellectuals who judge [the incidents of] the 1980s, do not exchange the place of martyr and executioner. The people of Iran were the subject of oppression in the 1980s. The terrorist *hypocrites* [MEK] and their supporters and the powers that created them and boasted about them treated the people of Iran with cruelty. The people of Iran were in a defensive posture."[55]

54 Khazali, Mehdi, interview with Dorr TV, August 28, 2016, http://www.dorrnews. com/?p=6261 also see, https://www.youtube.com/watch?v=J0okdDyHDMY

55 Ali Khamenei speech, Khamenei website, http://farsi.khamenei.ir/speech-content?id=36745

Ahmad Khatami, Tehran Friday Prayer Leader and member of the Assembly of Experts, July 21, 2017

"We see some people who on their websites switch the place of martyrs and murderers. Confronting them [imprisoned dissidents] and wiping out the *Monafeqin* [MEK] was one of the Imam's most righteous and valuable actions, and all of the people who complied with his edict should be awarded a Medal of Honor. ... Those who on their websites have switched the place of martyrs and murderers should repent and beg for forgiveness".[56]

Mohsen Rafiqdoost, former Minister of the IRGC, July 18, 2017

"If the arrested [MEK] elements were not executed, it was feared that they would make the revolution deviate... The wisest person in recent centuries was the Imam [Khomeini] who ordered that anyone who stands with his hypocritical choice should be killed. Today too, the order remains valid: if we find [MEK members], we will do the same to them."[57]

Mohammad-Reza Naqdi, Head of the Paramilitary Bassij Mostazafan Organization, Affiliated with the IRGC, August 30, 2016

In an interview with IRNA, Commander Mohammad-Reza Naqdi, said: "The executions of the *Monafeqin* that took place in 1988 for collaboration with Saddam and organizing to bring down the Islamic Republic of Iran were in full compliance with all judicial, religious, legal, Islamic, international and domestic standards... *Fatwas* issued by Imam [Khomeini] are based on solid religious and judicial foundations."[58]

---

56 Friday Prayers sermon, Ahmad Khatami, IRIB, July 21, 2017 http://www.iribnews.ir/fa/news/1727704/ https://www.youtube.com/watch?v=w68jLrWJ8i4

57 Interview with Mohsen Rafiqdoost, Mehr News Agency, July 18, 2017 http://www.mehrnews.com/news/4032488/

58 The execution of the hypocrites was completely right, Naqdi interview with IRNA, Fars News Agency, August 30, 2016, http://www.irna.ir/fa/News/82210739/

Ebrahim Raisi's Presidential Campaign, April - May 2017

In the weeks leading to the May 2017 presidential election, Ebrahim Raisi's campaign continuously sent out messages via the social network *Telegram* defending the 1988 massacre.

During a rally held on May 12, 2017, Yasser Mousavi, the Friday prayer leader in Varamin, with Raisi standing by his side introduced Raisi as such: "This grand figure who is standing next to me is proud to have executed the members of the [MEK]."[59]

Ebrahim Raisi implicated with the 1988 massacre of 30,000 political prisoners

Ali Razini, President of Branch 41 of the Supreme Court, July 2, 2017

Excerpts from an exclusive interview with Tasnim News Agency:

Tasnim: What are your views on the executions of 1988 of the *Monafeqin* [MEK] and the doubts that have been raised recently by some of their supporters?

Razini: "The officials involved in this affair were Messrs Nayyeri, Raisi, Reyshahri, Eshraqi and Pour-Mohammadi. You should put the question to them, since I was not involved in this affair. But in general I must say that if the Imam [Khomeini] wanted to issue death sentences without any considerations, as suggested by the counter-revolutionaries, then there would have been no need to set up commissions comprised of three persons. An announcement would have been made in the prisons to execute them [prisoners] then and there.

"They [the perpetrators] were religious judges who were not appointed by high ranking religious leaders; they were the same religious judges who had previously been appointed in various cities. For instance, the person who headed the revolutionary court in Semnan or Mashhad, the

---

59 Campaign speech of Ebrahim Raisi in Varamin, IRNA, May 12, 2017, http://www.irna.ir/fa/News/82526910

revolutionary prosecutor in the same city, plus the representative of the intelligence [ministry] in that city, who formed the three-man commissions. The trial sessions sometime lasted about an hour and in the end some were sentenced to death and some were not.

"Although the revolutionary courts at that time were managed by only one person, these courts were managed collectively and the decisions were made by consensus, although they could go by majority vote - that is two out of three votes. The sentences were only implemented when all three were united in the decision. In any case, all the procedures in 1988 were fair and conducted entirely in accordance with the law."[60]

Ali Fallahian, former Intelligence Minister, July 9, 2017

In an interview with the state-affiliated Tarikh On-line website (aired by the state-affiliated Aparat online video platform), Fallahian acknowledges that Khomeini's fatwa called for the eradication of all affiliates of the MEK. Defending the fatwa, Fallahian said that even MEK supporters whose only "crime" was to distribute the group's literature or buy bread or other provisions were found guilty of waging war on God and executed. Below is a translation of excerpts of Fallahian's interview[61].

Fallahian: "The Imam [Khomeini] decreed, 'At least execute those who say this and who maintain their belief. It doesn't make sense to release them.' Then some continued to object and moan that these people are this and that in prison, so it was decided that a committee be formed. Some people say that these officials handed down

Ali Fallahian, former Intelligence Minister defended the 1988 massacre in a TV interview

60 Executing Terrorist Hypocrites in 1988 was fair and legal (Farsi), Tasnim News Agency interview with Ali Razini, July 2, 2017. https://www.tasnimnews.com/fa/news/1396/04/11/1438610/

61 A 3-minute video of parts of his interview related to the massacre: https://www.youtube.com/watch?v=TXCtDzTqzHU; full interview: http://www.tarikhonline.com/public/video-share.php?id=206

Text on JVMI website: http://iran1988.org/ali-fallahian-former-intelligence-minister-iran-says-khomeini-ordered-execution-pmoi-affiliates-1988-massacre/

sentences for a collective massacre. They did no such thing. It was decided that this 3-man committee, whose members were from the [Intelligence] Ministry, the Prosecutor's office and knowledgeable judges, would evaluate to see if anyone should be pardoned from execution. That was the task of this committee; they were not tasked with issuing death sentences."

Tarikh Online *(*Interviewer): Excuse me, I want to make sure if I have understood correctly or not. The basis was that everyone would be executed, right?

Fallahian: "That's correct."

Tarikh Online: ... but this committee was tasked with pardoning some people from execution, right?

Fallahian: "They were supposed to be careful and follow up and speak with the person and check to see if he or she was really still maintaining his or her position. That was the criterion: standing firm."

Tarikh Online: What were the criteria for deciding if someone was maintaining his or her stand?

Fallahian: "Standing firm meant if someone said, I believe in the Organization [MEK], I don't believe in you, and if I am set free, I'd fight against you."

Tarikh Online: That would be crazy!

Fallahian: "They were crazy." (...)

Tarikh Online: .... So what was Mr. Montazeri's mistake?

Fallahian: "Mr. Montazeri had another problem, and he had differences with the Imam [Khomeini]. In the beginning, he too agreed [with Khomeini's position], but he came to believe that these executions would eventually lead to history judging against us and against Islam, so it would be better if we didn't do this so that in the future, when our enemies take up their pens, they would not write dreadful things about us. But the Imam said, 'No, you carry out your religious duties and don't wait for history's judgment'."

Tarikh Online: Were all those who were executed armed when they had been arrested?

Fallahian: "No."

Tarikh Online: Had they all carried out armed rebellion?

Fallahian: "They had all carried out armed rebellion, but many were arrested in team houses where we only found one or two guns or, for example, some were arrested on the streets and many of them were unarmed."

Tarikh Online: So how did this qualify as armed rebellion?

Fallahian: "Because they were part of that organization."

Tarikh Online: So, it's not necessary for that person to personally carry out that action?

Fallahian: "No. When someone is a member of a group or army, and when that army has taken up arms, then it makes no difference if that person is armed or unarmed."

Tarikh Online: Even if they were arrested with only a newspaper in their possession?

Fallahian: "Yes. They were part of that organization. They were prepared to carry out operations. Maybe one day someone goes and buys bread for the people in the team house, or someone might go provide other provisions..."

Tarikh Online: What if for example someone is not part of the operational force, is just part of their propaganda force?

Fallahian: "Well, that person is still part of them. When a unit is fighting, it has everything. It doesn't just have arms. They have support units."

Tarikh Online: Do they qualify as prisoners of war?

Fallahian: "No."

Ayatollah Mohammad Mohammadi Reyshahri, Member of the Assembly of Experts, former Minister of Intelligence, September 28, 2016

"Reyshahri condemned the release of the audio file, charging that the people behind it were trying to whitewash the image of the [MEK] at a time when the [MEK] is aligning with Iran's regional rival, Saudi Arabia.

He accused the people formerly in Montazeri's inner circle of either having a relationship with the [MEK] or having been penetrated by them."[62]

62 Montazeri audio is nothing new, Fars News Agency, *September 28, 2016*, http://www.farsnews.com/newstext.php?nn=13950606000666

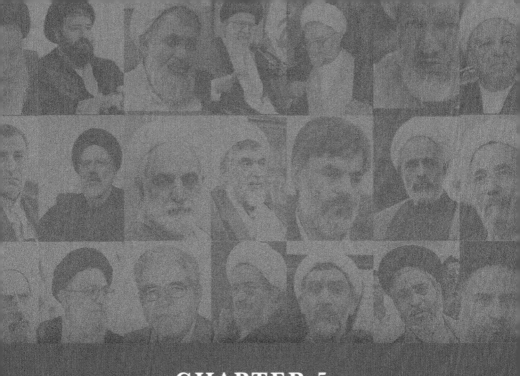

CHAPTER 5

The Chain of Command

❝… At Gohardasht prison, we were about 5,000 inmates. Those who made it with me to Evin were only 170. **❞**
— **Mohammad Zand**, *53, arrested on 26 July 1981.*
Total time spent in prison, 11 years.

At the end of July 1988, the Iranian regime's founder Khomeini issued a *fatwa* (religious decree) ordering the massacre of political prisoners. Death Committees were formed in more than 70 towns and cities to carry out the decree, each comprised of a religious judge, a prosecutor, and a representative of the Intelligence Ministry. Individuals such as the deputy prosecutor and heads of prisons cooperated with the Death Committees, and had a direct role in implementing the *fatwa*.[63] The religious judge and the prosecutor were appointed by the Supreme Judicial Council, headed by Abdul-Karim Moussavi Ardabili.

Ali Khamenei, currently the Iranian regime's Supreme Leader, and former president Ali Akbar Hashemi Rafsanjani, who was essentially the regime's number-two man in 1988, worked alongside Khomeini in executing the massacre. Khomeini's former designated successor, Hossein-Ali Montazeri, wrote in a letter that Khomeini sought counsel from these two individuals alone regarding his ominous decisions.

The highest decision-making body of the regime tasked with selecting the Supreme Leader's successor is the Assembly of Experts. Six members of the Assembly had a direct role in the massacre.[64]

The Judiciary is infested with officials responsible for the massacre. In addition to the Justice Minister, we have thus far identified 12 of the highest-ranking Judiciary officials as perpetrators of the massacre.

It is important to note that in the years since the 1988 massacre, the Justice Minister has always been chosen from among the perpetrators of the massacre—whether under the administrations of Rafsanjani, Khatami, Ahmadinejad or now Rouhani. These officials are Mohammad Esmail Shushtari (the Justice Minister during the Rafsanjani and Khatami administrations), Morteza Bakhtiari (Justice Minister in the Ahmadinejad administration), Mostafa Pour-Mohammadi (Justice Minister in the first term of

63 Christina Lamb, "Khomeini fatwa 'led to killing of 30,000 in Iran", *The Telegraph*, 04 February 2001, http://www.telegraph.co.uk/news/worldnews/middleeast/iran/1321090/ Khomeini-fatwa-led-to-killing-of-30000-in-Iran.html

64 Stop Fundamentalism, "Iran's Assembly of Experts admit to the 1988 massacre of thousands," *Stop Fundamentalism*, https://goo.gl/upZ1Bz

the Rouhani administration) and Alireza Avayi (appointed Justice Minister for Rouhani's second term).[65]

According to evidence obtained by the People's Mojahedin Organization of Iran (PMOI/MEK), most of the institutions of the Iranian regime are run by the perpetrators of the 1988 massacre. Information on 62 of the most senior officials responsible for the atrocity, some of whose names had remained secret for nearly three decades, were revealed by the Chair of the Foreign Affairs Committee of the National Council of Resistance of Iran (NCRI) at a press conference in Paris in September 2016. All of these figures currently hold key positions in various institutions of the regime, and were members of the "Death Committees" in Tehran and 10 other Iranian provinces.

Key decision-makers in 1988:

Ali Khamenei
1988: President
Current: Supreme Leader

Ali-Akbar Hashemi Rafsanjani
1988: Speaker of the Majlis (Parliament)
Deputy Commander of the Armed Forces
De facto no. 2 official after Khomeini
Current: Chairman of Expediency Council until his death in January 2017.

Ahmad Khomeini
1988: Son of Khomeini and his right-hand man, who hand-wrote the *fatwas* dictated by his father
Current: Deceased March 1995

---

65 "Mostafa Pour-Mohammadi appointed as Advisor to Iran's Judiciary Chief," *Justice for Victims of 1988 Massacre in Iran.* https://goo.gl/KtySEH

Abdul-Karim Moussavi Ardabili

1988: Chief Justice (later referred to as President of the Supreme Judicial Council)

Member of the Assembly of Experts

Current: Deceased in November 2016

Referring to the political prisoners, Moussavi Ardabili said, "They must all be executed… There will be no more of this sentencing and appeals." (Tehran radio, August 6, 1988)

He was first to receive Khomeini's *fatwa* and initially asked for clarification on its implementation. He was responsible for setting up the three-member commissions ordered by Khomeini to implement the executions.

Ayatollah Hossein-Ali Montazeri in his memoir recounts writing to Mousavi Ardabili, reminding him of his responsibility: "Weren't they your judges who condemned these prisoners to five or ten years in jail? Weren't you responsible? How is it that you telephone Haj Ahmad (Khomeini's son) and ask him, should we execute them (political prisoners) in Kashan or in Isfahan? You should have gone to the Imam (Khomeini) and told him, how can we execute someone who had been sentenced to five years and has been in jail for some time, and was not aware of the *Monafeqin's* (PMOI) activities? These people (serving prison terms) had not committed any new crimes for which we could try them (again)."

In 1988, the Supreme Judicial Council was the highest judicial authority in the country. It was dissolved in 1989, after the massacre. The council was comprised of five members: Chief Justice, the regime's highest judicial figure; the Prosecutor General; and three religious judges. The Supreme Judicial Council was responsible for setting up the three-member "Death Commissions" around the country and supervising their activities.

Mohammad Moussavi Khoeiniha

1988: Member of the Supreme Judicial Council; Prosecutor General

Current: Member of the Association of Combatant Clerics

In his capacity as Prosecutor General and member of the Supreme Judicial Council, he was directly involved in the implementation of the *fatwa*, including in setting up the three-member commissions known as the "Death Commissions."

During the US Embassy occupation in Tehran, he was Khomeini's representative among the "Muslim Student Followers of the Imam." He was appointed in 1985 as the country's Prosecutor General by Khomeini and remained in that post until 1989.

The French daily *Le Monde* wrote on 1 March 1989, "Imam Khomeini summoned the Revolutionary Prosecutor, Hojjatoleslam Mohammad Moussavi Khoeiniha, to instruct him that henceforth all PMOI members, whether held in prisons or anywhere else, must be executed for waging war on God. The executions followed summary trials. The trial was nothing more than a coercive process to extract confessions and forced repentance ..."

Morteza Moqtadaee

1988: Member and spokesperson of the Supreme Judicial Council

Current: Head of Qom Seminary; member of the Assembly of Experts

He joined the Judiciary in March 1979 when appointed as a judge in the revolutionary courts and served in Tehran, Qom, Khorramshahr, Abadan, Malayer and Zanjan.

Seyyed Mohammad Moussavi Bojnourdi

1988: Member and spokesperson of the Supreme Judicial Council

Current: Member of the Association of Combatant Clergy

He started working in 1979 in Khomeini's office in a section responsible for providing interpretation to legal issues according to *shari'a* rules. In 1981, he launched the Supreme Court for Judges upon Khomeini's order.

Seyyed Mohammad Hassan Marashi Shushtari
1988: Member and spokesperson of the Supreme Judicial Council
Current: Deceased 2009.

He was known to be one of the main founders of the Islamic Republic's Judiciary. He served in 1983 in Ahwaz, provincial capital of Khuzestan, first as a *shari'a* judge, and then as head of the revolutionary court until 1985. According to reliable sources, he was involved in trials and executions of opponents in Khuzestan province between 1983 and 1985.[66] After leaving the Supreme Judicial Council, he served in the National Supreme Court and was also a member of the Assembly of Experts.

Intelligence Ministry

According to Khomeini's *fatwa*, one of the members of the three-member "Death Commission" was drawn from the Ministry of Intelligence (MOIS). According to reliable witnesses, representatives of the MOIS played a major role in deciding the executions.

Ayatollah Montazeri wrote in his memoir "One of the judicial officers in Qom came to me and complained about the head of the Intelligence Department in Qom saying: 'The man says let us kill them off as quickly as we can and get rid of them once for all.' In his complaint, the judicial officer said: 'Let us at least look at the file and review the sentence.' The Intelligence officer replied: 'The Imam has issued the verdict; all we have to do is to ascertain that the prisoner is holding fast to his views'..."

Mohammad Mohammadi Reyshahri (A.K.A. Mohammad Mohammadi-Nik)
1988: Intelligence Minister; he appointed all representatives of the Ministry of Intelligence and Security (MOIS) in the "Death Commissions."
Current: Member of Assembly of Experts; Head of Shah AbdulAzim Endowment

Following the 1979 revolution he was head of Army Revolutionary Court. He was also Revolutionary Prosecutor and Special Prosecutor for the Clergy. He was the first Intelligence Minister when the post was established in 1984.

It is well documented that Reyshahri was personally involved in the massacre of political prisoners, just as the members of the "Death Commissions" he appointed.[67]

Ali Fallahian

1988: Deputy Intelligence Minister, responsible, along with the Minister, of setting up the three-member "Death Commissions" around the country.

Current: Member of the State Expediency Council

Before 1985 he was a *shari'a* judge in Khuzestan courts, where he was directly involved in executions. He replaced Reyshahri as Intelligence Minister from 1989 to 1997, and was a member of the Assembly of Experts from 2007 until 2016. Since November 7, 2007 he has been on the wanted list of Argentina's Judiciary for his role in the 1994 terrorist bombing of a Jewish community center in Buenos Aires. Interpol also issued a red notice for his role in the terrorist attack. [68]

There is also an international warrant for his arrest for having planned the assassination of Kurdish leaders at the Mikonos Restaurant in Berlin on September 17, 1992. In its April 10, 1997 ruling, a German court issued an international arrest warrant after declaring that the assassination had been ordered by him with the knowledge of Khamenei and Rafsanjani.[69]

In an interview with the state-affiliated *Tarikh Online website* (aired by the state-affiliated *Aparat* online video platform on 9 July 2017), Fallahian defended Khomeini's *fatwa*, saying that even PMOI supporters whose only "crime" was to distribute the group's literature or to buy bread or other provisions for them were found guilty of waging war on God and executed.[70]

67 "Iranian opposition exposes identities of officials responsible for 1988 massacre," *Track Persia*, https://goo.gl/9tUYZH

68 Keaten, Jamey "Interpol Puts 5 Iranians on Wanted List," *The Washington Post*, https://goo.gl/Sfi9hL

69 Afshari, Reza. *Human Rights in Iran: The Abuse of Cultural Relativism*. Pennsylvania: University of Pennsylvania Press, 2001

70 A 3-minute interview excerpt related to the massacre: https://www.youtube.com/watch?v=TXCt-DzTqzHU; full interview: http://www.tarikhonline.com/public/video-share.php?id=206

Mostafa Pourmohammadi

1988: Representative of Intelligence Ministry in the "Death Commission" in Tehran

Current: Minister of Justice for the first term of President Hassan Rouhani, Advisor to Chief of the Judiciary.

All those executed in Tehran and Karaj were sentenced to death under his ruling. In 2005, Human Rights Watch accused him of committing crimes against humanity for his role in the "Death Commission" and described him as a Minister of Murder.[71] Pour-Mohammadi was quoted on August 28, 2016 by the state-run *Tasnim news agency* as saying: "God commanded to show no mercy to the nonbelievers because they will not show mercy to you either and there should be no mercy to the [MEK] because if they could, they would spill your blood, which they did. ... We are proud to have carried out God's commandment with regard to the [Mojahedin] and to have stood with strength and fought against the enemies of God and the people."[72]

Javad Ali-Akbarian

1988: Deputy Minister of Intelligence [73]

Current: Deputy Head of Shah Abdul-Azim Endowment

In the early days after the Revolution, he was in charge of investigation in the office of the Revolutionary Prosecutor General and also served as Revolutionary Prosecutor in Gonbad and Isfahan. He was also in charge of the planning directorate, admin and finance of foreign intelligence of the Intelligence Ministry under Reyshahri. After leaving the Intelligence Ministry in 1989, he was appointed as deputy international head of the Islamic Culture and Communications Organization and vice-chair of this organization.

71 "Ministers of Murder: Iran's New Security Cabinet," *Human Rights Watch*, https://goo.gl/zoiHAN (accessed 17 November 2017

72 National Council of Resistance of Iran. *The 1988 Massacre of Political Prisoners in Iran: Time for the Truth, Justice, Reparation and Guarantees of Non-Recurrence.* September 12, 2017. https://goo.gl/XwiqTZ

73 Justice for Victims of 1988 Massacre in IRAN. 2017. https://iran1988.org/javad-ali-akbarian/

Gholam-Hossein Mohseni-Ejei

1988: The Judiciary's representative in the Intelligence Ministry

Current: First Vice Chief of the Judiciary since August 23, 2014, and Spokesperson for the Judiciary since September 16, 2010; member of the State Expediency Discernment Council

In 1988, he allegedly played an active role in the decision-making circle.[74] Human Rights Watch called for him to be put on trial for crimes against humanity committed during the mass executions.[75] He was Attorney General from 2009 to 2014,[76] and Intelligence Minister from 2005 until 2009. During the 2009 election, intelligence agents under his command were responsible for detention, torture and extraction of false confessions under duress from hundreds of activists, journalists, dissidents, and reformist politicians. In addition, political figures were coerced into making false confessions during interrogations using intimidation, blackmail, torture and the threatening of family members. In 2011, the European Union put him on its sanctions list for his role in serious violations of human rights and persecution of the opposition.[77]

74 Foreign Affairs Committee of the National Council of Resistance of Iran. *Crime Against Humanity: Indict Iran's Ruling Mullahs for Massacre of 30,000 Political Prisoners.* Auvers-sur-Oise: Foreign Affairs Committee of the National Council of Resistance of Iran, 2001.

75 "Ministers of Murder: Iran's New Security Cabinet," *Human Rights Watch,* https://goo.gl/zoiHAN

76 *Iran's Sacked Minister Named Top Prosecutor.* August 24, 2009. http://www.alarabiya.net/articles/2009/08/24/82760.html.

77 EUR-Lex: Access to European Union Law "Council Regulation (EU) No 359/2011 of 12 April 2011(Annex 1)" *Europa,* http://eur-lex.europa.eu/legal-content/EN/TXT/?uri=celex:32011D0235

Other Officials Who Played Key Roles in the Mass Executions

Majid Ansari
1988: Head of the State Prisons Organizations[78]
Current: Member of the State Expediency Council

Hossein-Ali Nayyeri
1988: Head of Tehran's Islamic Revolutionary Courts; *Shari'a* judge; and head of the "Death Commission" in Tehran [79]
Current: Head of the Supreme Disciplinary Court for Judges and Vice President of the Supreme Court

He was appointed as the Head of the "Death Commission" in Tehran upon Khomeini's order, issued on July 26, 1988. The "Death Commission" started its work in Tehran's Evin prison two days later. The commission operated in both Evin and Gohardasht prisons. It is reported that they used helicopters to commute rapidly between Evin and Gohardasht to issue death sentences.

Ali Mobasheri
1988: *Shari'a* Judge, acting as substitute to Hossein-Ali Nayyeri in the "Death Commission"
Current: Supreme Court judge

He joined the Judiciary in 1981 and was responsible for murdering the regime's opponents in Evin Prison. He reportedly described Assadollah

---

78 *Justice for Victims of 1988 Massacre in Iran (JVMI)*, https://iran1988.org/majid-ansari/
79 "Hossein-Ali Nayyeri", *Justice for Victims of 1988 Massacre in Iran (JVMI)*, https://iran1988.org/hossein-ali-nayyeri/

Lajevardi, the infamous governor of Evin Prison who was widely known as the "butcher of Evin", as a great man representing unique values.[80]

Morteza Eshraqi
1988: Tehran's Prosecutor; member of "Death Commission" in Tehran
Current: Lawyer practicing in Tehran

The task of issuing death sentences in Tehran was entrusted to him directly by Khomeini. Death sentences for thousands of prisoners affiliated with the MEK and other opponents were signed by him.[81]

Seyyed Ebrahim Rais al-Sadati (*A.K.A. Seyyed Ebrahim Raisi, Ibrahim Raeessi and Ebrahim Raeesi*)
1988: Tehran's Deputy Prosecutor; member of "Death Commission" in Tehran
Current: Head of Astan-e Qods Razavi Endowment Foundation; President of Governing Board of the Fifth Assembly of Experts; member of the State Expediency Discernment Council; 2017 presidential candidate.[82]

At the time of the 1988 mass executions, he headed the revolutionary court dealing with political prisoners. He instructed the arrests, torture, and execution of members of political groups. Raisi's campaign in the weeks leading to the May 2017 election continuously sent out messages via the social network Telegram defending the 1988 massacre. With Raisi standing by his side, Yasser Mousavi, the Friday prayer' leader in Varamin, said at a Raisi campaign rally on 12 May 2017: "This grand figure standing next to me is proud to have executed the members of the MEK".[83]

80 National Council of Resistance of Iran, Foreign Affairs Committee, *Crime Against Humanity*, 2001, https://www.scribd.com/document/2469298/Crime-Against-Humanity

81 Ibid.

82 Presidential Elections in Iran, U.S. Representative Office, Presidential Elections in Iran: Changing Faces; Status Quo Policies, page 64, https://www.amazon.com/gp/product/1944942041

83 Campaign speech of Ebrahim Raisi in Varamin, IRNA, May 12, 2017, http://www.irna.ir/fa/News/82526910

Mohammad Esmail Shushtari

1988: Head of the state Prisons Organization; member of "Death Commission" in Tehran [84]

Current: Head of the Presidency's Inspectorate Office until August 2016. Retired

He served as Iran's Minister of Justice for 16 years under Ali-Akbar Hashemi Rafsanjani and Mohammad Khatami.

Ali Razini

1988: Head of the Judicial Organization of the Armed Forces; member of "Death Commission" in Tehran[85]

Current: Head of the 41st Branch of the Supreme Court

Khomeini assigned him on July 24, 1988 to "set up special courts to deal with war offences in all war zones and deal with offenders in accordance with *shari'a*, disregarding rules and regulations that can be restrictive and troublesome; and to ensure that any act that may lead to the failure of the Islamic front is punished by death."

Seyyed Hossein Mortazavi Zanjani

1988: Governor of Evin Prison; member of "Death Commission" in Tehran

Current: Businessman; owner of a publicity firm

He began his career in the cultural section of Evin Prison, working under the "butcher of Evin," Assadollah Lajevardi.[86] After Lajevardi's

84 "Mohammad Esmail Sushtari", *"Justice for Victims of 1988 Massacre in Iran (JVMI)"*, https://iran1988.org/mohammad-esmail-shushtari/

85 *Justice for Victims of 1988 Massacre in Iran (JVMI)*, https://goo.gl/XQ9meF

86 Jack Anderson and Dale Van Atta, Iranian Prison Horror, The Washington Post, January 14, 1990, https://www.washingtonpost.com/archive/opinions/1990/01/14/iranian-prison-horror/dcc84966-4289-497c-a168-8ba3bea4566d/

departure in 1985, he was first appointed as Governor of Gohardasht (Rajai-Shahr) Prison and then Evin Prison.[87]

Alireza Avayi

1988: Prosecutor; member of the Dezful "Death Commission" [88]

Current: Minister of Justice (from September 2017); Head of the Presidency's Inspectorate Office (until September 2017)

After receiving Khomeini's *fatwa*, he was the main person in charge of executions in the UNESCO Prison in Dezful. (A school facility built during the Shah's regime by UNESCO to help children, it was transformed into a prison operating under the same name by the current regime.) He has been described by witnesses as one of the cruelest murderers of the 1988 mass executions. According to eyewitness accounts, teenage prisoners were executed in the area behind the prison yard.

The European Union sanctioned Alireza Avayi for human rights violations in April 2011. The EU described him as "Director of the special investigations office. Until July 2016 deputy Minister of Interior and head of the Public register. Advisor to the Disciplinary Court for Judges since April 2014. Former President of the Tehran Judiciary. As President of the Tehran Judiciary he has been responsible for human rights violations, arbitrary arrests, denials of prisoners' rights and an increase in executions."[89]

In another measure in October 2011, the EU imposed further sanctions.[90]

87 National Council of Resistance of Iran, Foreign Affairs Committee, *Crime Against Humanity*, 2001, https://goo.gl/Q7TYZK

88 Justice for Victims of 1988 Massacre in Iran (JVMI), https://goo.gl/SPGxp7

89 Council Implementing Regulation (EU) 2017/685 of 11 April 2017 implementing Regulation (EU) No 359/2011 concerning restrictive measures directed against certain persons, entities and bodies in view of the situation in Iran. http://eur-lex.europa.eu/legal-content/EN/TXT/?uri=uriserv:OJ.L_.2017.099.01.0010.01.ENG

90 Council of the European Union, "Council Implementing Regulation (EU) No 1002/2011 of 10 October 2011 Implementing Article 12(1) of Regulation (EU) No 359/2011 Concerning Restrictive Measures Directed Against Certain Persons, Entities and Bodies in View of the Situation in Iran," Official Journal of the European Union, October 10, 2011, page 2. http://eur-lex.europa.eu/LexUriServ/LexUriServ.do?uri=OJ:L:2011:267:0001:0006:EN:PDF

CHAPTER 6
The Killings Continue

" *Crimes against international law are committed by men, not by abstract entities, and only by punishing individuals who commit such crimes can the provisions of international law be enforced.* "

—Judgment of the Nuremberg Tribunal,
September 30 & October 1, 1946

In his disclosed audio tape, Montazeri tells the former death committee members: "The greatest crime committed during the reign of the Islamic Republic, for which history will condemn us, has been committed by you. Your (names) will be etched in the annals of history as criminals."[91]

Montazeri details some of the most abhorrent aspects of the murders, such as executions of pregnant women and young girls, as well as the condemnation of people whose support for the MEK consisted only of reading their publications. He adds, "Executing these people while there have been no new activities [by the prisoners] means that...the entire judicial system has been wrong."[92]

The targets of Montazeri's rebuke, Mostafa Pour Mohammadi, representative of the Ministry of Intelligence (MOIS) in Evin Prison; Hossein Ali Nayyeri, shari'a judge; Morteza Eshraghi, public prosecutor; and Ebrahim Raisi, deputy prosecutor, are all veteran officials of the theocratic regime. Their careers were and remain interwoven with former and current top officials, such as Mir Hossein Mousavi, the previous Prime Minister of Iran from 1981 to 1989 and leader of the self-proclaimed "moderate" Green Movement; Ali Akbar Hashemi Rafsanjani, then-Speaker of the Parliament who in later years also proclaimed himself a "moderate"; Ali Khamenei, then-President and now Supreme Leader; and Hassan Rouhani, appointed by Khomeini as First Secretary of the Supreme National Security Council in the wake of the killings in 1989.

Such was the brutal scale of the massacre that Montazeri laments, "The people are now revolted by the system of absolute rule of the supreme religious leader."[93] By contrast, none of the regime's other top officials, then or now, have ever spoken out in condemnation of the carnage.

When the tape surfaced on August 9, 2016, Tehran could not simply disregard Montazeri's recorded words, which were uttered as if the dead were speaking from the grave.[94] Although he was eased out of the regime as a result of his dissent, he was such a prominent figure in 1988 and in

91 "Audio transcript of Iran officials' remarks about the 1988 massacre," *Justice for the Victims of the 1988 Massacre in Iran*, goo.gl/McdqHX.

92 Ibid,.

93 Ibid,.

94 Ibid,.

religious circles that from the time of the tape's release to the time of this writing, there has been renewed public discussion of the mass murders. The conversation went viral on the Internet, and particularly escalated when Ebrahim Raisi, the same man named in the tape as a member of Tehran's death committee, was announced in April 2017 as a candidate for the May 2017 presidential election.[95] His candidacy was strongly favored by Supreme Leader Ali Khamenei.

The tape only underscores an ugly truth that was already known to anyone who had looked but ignored the truth in order to deal with or appease Tehran: many of the main perpetrators of the mass killings still hold high-level positions in the Iranian regime. Ebrahim Raisi was the clerical regime's prosecutor general until almost a year ago, when he was appointed by Khamenei as custodian of an immensely wealthy foundation that is one of the most important political and economic institutions in the clerical regime.[96]

Hossein-Ali Nayyeri, also a member of the death committee, is the current head of the Supreme Disciplinary Court for Judges.[97]

Mostafa Pour-Mohammadi was the Justice Minister in President Hassan Rouhani's first cabinet.[98] Shortly after his public exposure on August 28, 2016, Pourmohammadi adamantly defended his prominent role in the mass murders. After a public outcry, Rouhani replaced him as Justice Minister with Alireza Avayi, also a member of a Death Committee.

The Late Lord Eric Avebury, Member of the UK House of Lords and former Vice-chairman of the British Parliamentary Human Rights Group, wrote: "If those responsible for this crime against humanity go free, a terrible

95 Carol Morello and Erin Cunningham, "The nuclear deal takes center stage as Iran's election campaign gets underway," *The Washington Post*, 27 April 2017, https://www.washingtonpost.com/world/middle_east/the-nuclear-deal-takes-center-stage-as-irans-election-campaign-gets-underway/2017/04/27/2f9377d4-2a97-11e7-9081-f5405f56d3e4_story.html.

96 Gareth Smyth, "Iran's Leader Picks Ebrahim Raisi to head powerful foundation," *The Guardian*, 9 March 2016, https://www.theguardian.com/world/2016/mar/09/irans-supreme-leader-key-appointment-ebrahim-raisi-mashhad-foundation.

97 *Justice for the Victims of the 1988 Massacre in Iran*, https://iran1988.org/hossein-ali-nayyeri/.

98 "Mostafa Pourmohammadi," *Islamic State of Iran Crime Research Center*, http://isicrc.org/mostafa-pourmohammadi/.

injustice will have been done to the victims, their families, and the survivors of the mass executions. The cause of international justice and universality of jurisdiction over crimes against humanity will have been seriously impaired."[99]

Jafar Kazemi, executed in 2011

We can now observe that such persecution without just prosecution has encouraged the clerical regime, which is now recognized as the world leader in the number of executions per capita.[100] Amnesty International's Global Report on death sentences and executions in 2016 states that Iran carried out 66% of all executions in the Middle East in 2016.[101]

Indeed, Iran's pattern of executions has been prevalent throughout the twenty-first century. Between 2009 and 2010, the Iranian regime arrested and executed multiple political prisoners and alleged members of the MEK. Included among these individuals were Jafar

Mohammad Haj Aghaee, executed in 2011 for his participation in 2009 uprising

Kazemi and Mohammad Haj Aghaee, who were arrested after the 2009 elections and were "convicted of *moharebeh* (enmity against God)" for their

99 National Council of Resistance of Iran Foreign Affairs Committee, *Crimes Against Humanity* (France, Foreign Affairs Committee of the National Council of Resistance of Iran, 2001), iii.

100 Lynch, Colum. "Iran Wins World Record for Most Executions Per Capita." *Foreign Policy*. October 27, 2015, http://foreignpolicy.com/2015/10/27/rouhani-zarif-state-department-human-rightsiran-wins-world-record-for-most-executions-per-capita/.

101 "The Death penalty in 2016: Facts and figures." *Amnesty International*, 11 April 2017, https://www.amnesty.org/en/latest/news/2017/04/death-penalty-2016-facts-and-figures/

associations with the MEK.[102] They were sentenced to death in 2010. Tehran summarily executed them in January of 2011. Similarly, Ali Saremi was executed in 2010 after four separate arrests and a total of twenty-four years of imprisonment. The Iranian government stated that he was charged with "publicity activities against the sacred rule of Islamic Republic" as a result of his involvement with the MEK. As reported by the NCRI in December of 2010, Sarami was subjected to brutal torture techniques before being executed.

A fourth example of this pattern can be found in the case of Gholamreza Khosravi, who was

Ali Saremi, executed in 2010 for association with the MEK after 24 years of imprisonment

Gholamreza Khosravi with his son

Gholamreza Khosravi in prison, days before his execution in 2014

102 Appeal for Iranian man rejected, Human Rights & Democracy for Iran, August 5, 2010, https://www.iranrights.org/library/document/1481/iran-further-information-appeal-for-iranian-man-rejected-jafar-kazemi

arrested in 2007 on the same charges of "enmity against God" and sentenced to death in 2010. Despite pleas from Amnesty International, which stated that Khosravi had not been given a fair trial, he was executed in 2014.[103]

These executions drew outcry from across the globe. In 2010, U.S. Secretary of State Hillary Clinton condemned the acts, stating, "The United States is deeply concerned that Iran continues to deny its citizens their civil rights and intimidate and detain those Iranians who seek to hold their government accountable."[104] Before the deaths of Jafar Kazemi and Mohammad Haj Aghaee, Secretary Clinton expressed her concern and urged the regime to halt the executions, claiming that the two prisoners were being persecuted simply "for exercising their right to free expression after the June 2009 elections."[105] NCRI president-elect Mrs. Maryam Rajavi spoke out against the injustices: "This great crime only reflects the regime's inability and frustration in face of the resolute Iranian youths and members of MEK who are determined to overthrow the clerical rule and establish freedom and the rule of people in Iran."[106] A 2014 Reuters article quoted Amnesty International's deputy director for the Middle East and Africa, Hassiba Hadj Saharoui, who described Khosravi's execution by saying "Yet again Iranian authorities are about to execute a man who did not even receive a fair trial in total disregard of both international law and the Iranian law."[107]

Today's Iran has certainly been no more commendable regarding justice and human rights. The March 2017 report by the UN Secretary General on the situation of human rights in Iran states: "The Secretary-General

103 "Gholamreza Khosravi Savadjani Executed", *Amnesty International* 3 June 2014, https://www.amnesty.org/en/documents/mde13/030/2014/en/

104 Preeti Aroo, "Clinton to Iran: Don't execute your citizens; respect human rights," *Foreign Policy*, 12 August 2010

105 Hillary Rodham Clinton press statement, Urging Iran to Respect the Fundamental Freedoms of its Citizens, 10 August 2010, https://2009-2017.state.gov/secretary/20092013clinton/rm/2010/08/145857.htm

106 NCRI statement, "Political Prisoner Ali Sarami Hanged after 24 Years Incarceration," 28 December 2010, https://www.ncr-iran.org/en/ncri-statements/ashraf-liberty/9550-political-prisoner-ali-sarami-hanged-after-24-years-incarceration

107 "Amnesty says Iranian dissident faces imminent execution," *Reuters*, 31 May, 2014, https://ca.reuters.com/article/topNews/idCAKBN0EB0VX20140531

is alarmed at the number of individuals who were executed in Iran and of the death sentences handed down… Two mass executions were conducted in 2016. On 5 August alone, 20 people belonging to the Kurdish minority were executed for purported terrorism-related offences, although concerns had been expressed by the Special Rapporteur on the situation of human rights in Iran and by the United Nations High Commissioner for Human Rights regarding the fairness of their trials."[108]

The report adds, "The Secretary-General remains concerned about a number of death penalty cases with a political dimension. Several individuals were reportedly executed in political cases and non-violent economic crimes during the second half of 2016, following proceedings that reportedly did not comply with international norms regarding fair trial and due process provided for in article 14 of the International Covenant on Civil and Political Rights, to which the Islamic Republic of Iran is a State party."

There is no reason why Iranian authorities should take the International Covenant on Civil and Political Rights or any other international law seriously; as long as criminals like Raisi, Nayyeri, Pour-Mohammadi, and their accomplices in the ruling regime remain not only unpunished, but in positions of power. A regime which, after intense vetting, proudly approved a mass murderer like Raisi as a candidate in a presidential election has absolutely no capacity for talks on human rights, no respect for international laws, and no prospects for any change.

108 Secretary General of the United Nations, "Situation of human rights in the Islamic Republic of Iran," *United Nations Human Rights Council*, 13 March 2017

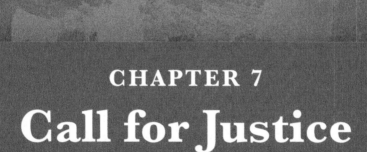

CHAPTER 7
Call for Justice

❝*What happened in 1988 was a crime against humanity.
Crimes against humanity are of a special hideousness.
They cannot be forgotten, and they cannot be forgiven.***❞**
—Geoffrey Robertson,
United Nations Plaza, 2016

The Iranian Regime used the pretext of judicial "retrials" as a cover for the 1988 mass execution of political prisoners. The proceedings, however, bore little resemblance to any form of modern, respectable judicial practices. Instead, they were systematic interrogation sessions designed to force political prisoners to denounce their political views. Those who did not kneel and kiss the ring of the regime were executed.

To cover up their crimes against humanity, the regime threatened the friends and families of the victims against any acknowledgements, let alone complaints, about what had taken place. Families could not hold memorial services or funerals. Yet, the Iranian people persisted. Every year, families held gatherings in Khavaran Cemetery in Tehran, the presumed location of the mass graves housing the 1988 victims, despite intimidation and threats by the regime.[109] Unfortunately, the regime is notorious for responding to innocent acts of remembrance with cruel and unforgiving violence. Ali Saremi, a political activist and MEK supporter, was arrested and executed for paying tribute to the lives lost.[110] Even stones and flowers left at the presumed graves were interpreted

Families gather in Khavaran cemetary every year to pay tribute to the victims of 1988 massacre

Ali Saremi, an MEK supporter, executed for paying tribute to the lives lost in Khavaran cemetary

---

109 "Families of Executed Political Prisoners Barred From Gathering In Tehran," Radio Farda, 29 August 2008, https://www.rferl.org/a/Commemoration_Barred_In_Tehran/1194984.html.

110 "Political prisoner Ali Saremi hanged after 24 years incarceration," *The National Council of Resistance of Iran*, 28 December 2010, https://www.ncr-iran.org/en/ncri-statements/ashraf/9550-political-prisoner-ali-sarami-hanged-after-24-years-incarceration.

as potentially incriminating "evidence" by the regime, and destroyed immediately.

In the aftermath, the MEK and NCRI transmitted intelligence regarding the crimes to UN authorities and human rights organizations. But the true extent and details of the crimes committed were only partially known, even by MEK and NCRI personnel, who had the only connections to survivors' firsthand accounts. Even today, much of what happened is unaccounted for. Official facts and figures are non-existent.

Professor Kazem Rajavi, who was later assassinated by the Iranian regime in 1990 in Geneva, in particular, brought the regime's crimes to the attention of the UN Human Rights Commission with the objective of forming a UN fact-finding commission that could lead to justice for the Iranian people.[111] His efforts were rewarded with a hard-won mention in the resolution passed by the UNHRC in 1989, "... Expresses its grave concern at the reports of a wave of summary executions in the period from July to December 1988."[112] But no fact-finding commission was established.

Professor Kazem Rajavi paved the way for UN resolutions about the human rights violations in Iran

The UNHRC's Special Representative to the 1989 session, reminded the UN experts of his earlier report about "information he received in September 1988 alleging that a large number of prisoners, members of various opposition groups, had been executed during the months of July, August and September 1988. Since that date, the Special Representative has continued receiving persistent reports about a wave of executions of political prisoners..."

111 Richard Bernstein, "Iranian at UN: No Room on Agenda," *The New York Times*, 7 December 1983, http://www.nytimes.com/1983/12/07/world/iranian-at-un-no-room-on-agenda.html.

112 United Nations, Human Rights Commission, "Report on the human rights situation in the Islamic Republic of Iran," E/CN. 4/1989/26, 26 January 1989, http://repository.un.org/handle/11176/178831.

In addition, he said, he had "received hundreds of petitions and letters from private individuals around the world, including members of parliament from Australia, France, Germany, Ireland, and the United Kingdom of Great Britain and Northern Ireland, as well as members of the European Parliament from several countries, and trade-union and church officials, expressing deep concern at the alleged wave of executions and calling for United Nations intervention to bring such executions to a halt."

The Special Representative noted, "Statements by several high-ranking officials were published by the Iranian news media to the effect that members of opposition groups should be dealt with severely, but there was no official acknowledgement of the wave of executions. Nevertheless, reports have been received according to which people witnessed large numbers of bodies being buried in shallow graves in the area of Behesht-e-Zahra cemetery in Tehran, where political prisoners are usually buried, and in other parts of the country..."[113]

Those reports had been transmitted by the Special Rapporteur on Arbitrary Executions, whose efforts focused on cables he had "... sent to the Government of the Islamic Republic of Iran on 26 August, 14 September, 11 and 15 November, 1, 8, 9, 20 and 23 December 1988 concerning allegations that since July 1988 a large number of prisoners, said to be members or supporters of groups or organizations opposing the Government, had been executed and several others were facing imminent execution in various parts of the country.... In view of persistent reports received that several thousand persons had been executed without trial or with a trial of a summary nature."

The Special Rapporteur went on to cite report after report, date after date, victim after victim, in each case appealing "to the Government to ensure that the right to life of the above-mentioned persons was protected as provided for in the International Covenant on Civil and Political Rights. He also requested information on the above-mentioned cases as well as any information on the fate of the persons mentioned in his previous cables..."

113 Ibid..

His report concluded with the simple, yet telling statement: "At the time of preparation of the present report, no reply had been received from the Government of the Islamic Republic of Iran."[114]

International Concern

There have been numerous international demands for further prevention of human rights abuses, most prominently by Amnesty International and the United Nations, and numerous proposals to the United Nation's General Assembly outlining the Iranian regime's human rights abuses. One prevalent issue concerns the non-binding legal nature of the Charter on Citizens' Rights, proposed by the Iranian regime's executive branch. This charter was still "draft legislation" containing no specific enforcement guarantee.[115] In other words, the Iranian regime does not currently hold itself to any self-enforced standards of human rights. This of course means that massacres, like the prison massacre of 1988, could very well reoccur in the future. This is particularly troubling in the context of the United Nations Declaration of Human Rights, signed by the state of Iran in 1948, before the Ayatollahs were in power. The theocratic regime, therefore, never officially accepted international standards of human rights, as evident by the current conditions in Iran today.

Ms. Asma Jahangir, special rapporteur on the situation of human rights in Iran, provided insight into the regime's lack of human rights accountability, specifically on the rights of women and the press, in

Asma Jahangir Special Rapporteur on the situation of human rights in Iran highlights the continued political killings in Iran

114 United Nations, Economic and Social Council, "Report by the Special Rapporteur, Mr. S. Amos Wako, pursuant to Economic and Social Council resolution 1988/38," E/CN. 4/1989/25, 6 February 1989, https://documents-dds-ny.un.org/doc/UNDOC/GEN/ G89/104/02/PDF/G8910402.pdf?OpenElement.

115 Radio Farda, November 4, 2017, https://www.radiofarda.com/a/Irani-an-mps-formed-new-Parliamentary-fraction-to-pursue-civil-rights/28835277.html

her 2017 report: "Equally disturbing and no less chilling are the reports that I receive of violations against the rights to freedom of expression, opinion, information and the press. As of June 2017, at least 12 journalists, as well as 14 bloggers and social media activists were either in detention or had been sentenced for their peaceful activities. Other media workers report being subjected to interrogation, surveillance, and other forms of harassment and intimidation.

"I welcomed the pledges made by President Rouhani to address the rights of women in Iran, and noted the commitment made by the State to the Sustainable Development Goals, including Goal 5 on achieving gender equality and empowerment. However, the vehement reaction to the social media campaigns protesting against mandatory dress codes; the arrest of individuals for allegedly reading and spreading feminist literature; the ongoing ban prohibiting women from watching sporting events in stadiums in contravention to the Charter; and exclusion of women from certain occupations and positions suggest much remains to be done to realise these commitments. I call upon the Government to address these concerns in practice, and in legislation through ratifying the Convention on the Elimination of All Forms of Discrimination against Women and to repeal all laws and policies that discriminate against women and girls."[116]

Amnesty International has targeted the regime's reprisals against families and destruction of mass grave sites: "The Iranian authorities must urgently stop the destruction of a mass grave in the southern city of Ahvaz said Amnesty International today, launching a campaign to urge authorities to protect the site, where dozens of prisoners killed during a wave of mass extrajudicial executions in August and September 1988 are buried."[117]

116 Human Rights & Democracy for Iran, Statement of Asma Jahangir, Special Rapporteur on Human Rights in Iran, to UN General Assembly, 25 October 2017, https://www.iran-rights.org/library/document/3260

117 "Iran: Campaign to stop destruction of mass grave of those killed in 1988 prison massacre," *Amnesty International*, 4 September 2017, https://www.amnesty.org/en/latest/news/2017/09/iran-campaign-to-stop-destruction-of-mass-grave-of-those-killed-in-1988-prison-massacre/.

A Failure to Act

To the dismay of the Iranian people, the justice-seeking process has been repeatedly interrupted by political and economic reservations. As such, the perpetrators of the 1988 massacre have enjoyed impunity for nearly 30 years, and remain in official government positions, despite the adoption of the Statute for the International Criminal Court in Rome on July 17, 1998.[118]

Geoffrey Robertson conducted a study on the 1988 massacre of political prisoners in Iran, which was published in June 2011. In his report, he asks, "Does a massacre that happened twenty years ago, at the very end of an eight-year war that claimed about a million lives, and which targeted prisoners who were in some way sympathetic to terrorists, communists or Iraq (the

Geoffrey Robertson QC conducted a study about the 1988 massacre in Iran

national enemy) really matter today? More than ever, in my view. International law is the prisoner's only succor in times of war, when states are often especially prone to exploit popular hostility and unleash the lynch mob. Convicts make for particularly useful scapegoats, and if the temptation to slaughter them is to be kept at bay in the future, notorious cases in the recent past must be exposed and expiated."[119]

Geoffrey Robertson, is former judge of the UN Special Court for Sierra Leone. On May 30, 2012, *The New York Times* reported that Charles Taylor, former Liberian president, was convicted of atrocities he committed in neighboring Sierra Leonne.[120]

118 "Summary of the Key Provisions of the ICC Statute," *Human Rights Watch*, 1 December 1998, https://www.hrw.org/news/1998/12/01/summary-key-provisions-icc-statute.

119 Human Rights & Democracy for Iran, e Massacre of Political Prisoners in Iran, 1988, Report of an Inquiry Conducted by Geoffrey Robertson QC, https://www.iranrights. org/library/document/1380/the-massacre-of-political-prisoners-in-iran-1988-report-of-an-inquiry

120 Marlise Simons and J. David Goodman, "Ex-Liberian Leader Gets 50 Years for War Crimes," *The New York Times*, 30 May 2012, http://www.nytimes.com/2012/05/31/world/africa/charles-taylor-sentenced-to-50-years-for-war-crimes.html.

In a speech at United Nations plaza in 2016, Robertson elaborated on the Montazeri audiotape release: "The Geneva conventions in 1949, the basis of international law, makes it an international crime to kill a prisoner. Since the Second World War, there have been 3 heinous and hideous examples of that. The first was the Japanese army that war marched, death marched 7,000 American soldiers to their death in 1946. What happened to the Japanese commanders who ordered that crime? They were tried, and they were convicted and they were executed.

"The second example was Srebrenica, in 1992, when 7,000 Muslim men and boys were killed. What happened to those commanders who gave the orders to Millovech and Karadzic? They are on trial at The Hague at this time. They were punished and will be punished.

"The third, the worst example, came in 1988 when thousands of upon thousands of prisoners who were in the first place members of the MEK, then they came for the atheists, for the communists, for the liberals, people who were in prison for their politics, many of them had served their sentence, they'd been arrested in 1981 and were being held in prison although they finished their sentence, were killed, monstrously, and this is why, this dreadful act has never been punished. It has never even been investigated apart from an investigation that I did at the behest of the Boroumand foundation a few years ago...What happened in 1988 was a crime against humanity. Crimes against humanity are of a special hideousness. They cannot be forgotten, and they cannot be forgiven. There is a duty by the world community, represented by the United Nations, to take action... It's perfectly possible for the UN and Security Council to set up an international ad hoc tribunal, like the one in Sierra Leone, that I was president of, like the one in Cambodia, to investigate and punish those who are guilty of the 1988 prison massacres. That is the duty that is on the Security Council. For crimes against humanity, there must be an investigation, there must be punishment."[121]

The damning avalanche of evidence set free with the Montazeri audiotape leak brought about the unwelcome nationwide coverage the regime so

121 Geoffrey Robertson, OIAC, *"Sir Geoffrey Robertson speech at UN Rally—Sept 20, 2016,"* Youtube.com, 13:36 minutes, 20 September 2016, https://www.youtube.com/watch?v=Fb-WhFqThcg.

dreads. There are those in power who proudly admit to having taken part in the mass murders, assuming they are untouchable, and there are those who took part, but deny their participation. The public, and even some officials within the clerical establishment, immediately demanded an explanation and apology from the perpetrators.

It has been over a year, but the political and social tumult persists, and every day new details of the 1988 massacre surface. Victims' families in some cases finally have the courage and motivation to step forward, and relay untold stories of their loved ones and the mass graves that house them. A new hope has revived the hearts of many families, current political prisoners, and activists to revitalize the justice-seeking campaign for the victims of the 1988 massacre. Relatives of the executed have started writing to the UN Secretary General and the UN Special Rapporteur on Human Rights, calling for justice. Similarly, current political prisoners have raised their voices against these crimes against humanity from the depths of the regime's dungeons. In one case, Maryam Akbari-Monfared, now in Evin prison, filed a complaint with the Prosecution Office in Tehran in a symbolic act, asking for a trial of those responsible for the massacre of her sister and brother in summer 1988.[122]

Political activists seek the establishment of a Special Court for the Iranian regime, perhaps fashioned on the model of the United Nations Special Court for Sierra Leone and related bodies.

Members of the United States Congress increased their pressure on the Iranian regime, when the House Foreign Affairs Committee introduced H.Res.188, on March 9, 2017, which both acknowledged the atrocities committed by the regime, and set in motion preliminary

Chairman Michael McCaul introduced a House resolution on the 1988 massacre in Iran

---

122 "Political prisoner, Maryam Akbari Monfared, seeks justice over Iran's 1988 massacre." *Justice for Victims of 1988 Massacre in Iran,* 2016, https://iran1988.org/maryam-akbari-monfared/.

demands for justice. The resolution was introduced with large bipartisan support including Representatives Michael McCaul (R-TX), Edward Royce (R-CA), Eliot Engel (D-NY), Pete Sessions (R-TX), William Keating (D-MA), Tom McClintock (R-CA-4), Brad Sherman (D-CA), and Don Young (R-AK). The legislation details the tortur-

Chairman Ed Royce (left) and ranking member Eliot Engel co-sponsor the resolution on the 1988 massacre

ous, rapid, and inhumane way that thousands of political prisoners were executed in 1988:

"Whereas the killings were carried out on the orders of a judge, an official from the Ministry of Intelligence, and a state prosecutor, known to the prisoners as Death Commissions which undertook proceedings in a manner designed to eliminate the regime's opponents;

"Whereas those personally responsible for these mass executions include senior officials serving in the current Government of Iran;

"Whereas prisoners were reportedly brought before the commissions and briefly questioned about their political affiliation, and any prisoner who refused to renounce his or her affiliation with groups perceived as enemies by the regime was then taken away for execution;

"Whereas the victims included thousands of people, including teenagers and pregnant women, imprisoned merely for participating in peaceful street protests and for possessing political reading material, many of whom had already served or were currently serving prison sentences;

"Whereas prisoners were executed in groups, some in mass hangings and others by firing squad, with their bodies disposed of in mass graves..."

Ultimately, the resolution concludes with two critical demands, calling on:

"(1) the Administration and U.S. allies to condemn the massacre and pressure the Iranian government to provide detailed information to the victims' families about their loved ones and their final resting places.

"(2) The United Nations (U.N.) Special Rapporteur on the human rights situation in Iran and the U.N. Human Rights Council to create a Commission of Inquiry to investigate the massacre, gather evidence, identify the perpetrators, and bring them to justice."[123]

Meanwhile, Canadian lawmakers urged their own government on October 6, 2016, to formally address the 1988 massacre.[124] This was a particularly significant development, as, in recent years, Canada has taken the initiative on drafting and introducing the UN resolutions censuring Iran for human rights violations.

A similar call was made by dozens of members of both houses of the British Parliament, who issued a statement supporting the international movement to obtain justice for the massacre victims.[125]

It is time that the victims receive the justice they so rightfully deserve. They have a very clear message: justice for the 1988 massacre. Over the past decades, there have been public condemnations and recognition, yet there have been no concrete consequences. This must change. We cannot continue to allow a warring state, with no obligation to protect human rights, to go unchecked. In the words of the United Nations, at the very least "the

---

123 U.S. House Committee on Foreign Affairs, 115th Congress, 1st Session, *H.RES.188, Condemning the Government of the Islamic Republic of Iran for the 1988 massacre of political prisoners and calling for justice for the victims*, Washington, Government Printing Office, 2017, https://www.congress.gov/bill/115th-congress/house-resolution/188.

124 "Prominent Politicians and lawmakers urge Canadian Government to demand UN inquiry into hideous massacre of political prisoners in Iran in 1988," *The National Council of Resistance of Iran*, 7 October 2017, https://www.ncr-iran.org/en/news/human-rights/21252-prominent-politicians-and-lawmakers-urge-canadian-government-to-demand-un-inquiry-into-hideous-massacre-of-political-prisoners-in-iran-in-1988.

125 "British parliamentarians call for investigation into 1988 Iranian massacre," *TrackPersia.com*, 6 October 2017, http://www.trackpersia.com/british-parliamentarians-call-investigation-1988-iranian-massacre/.

families of the victims have a right to know the truth about these events and the fate of their loved ones without risking reprisal. They have the right to a remedy, which includes the right to an effective investigation of the facts and public disclosure of the truth; and the right to reparation."[126]

126 "Report of the Special Rapporteur on the situation of human rights in the Islamic Republic of Iran," (A/72/322), 14 August 2017, http://undocs.org/A/72/322

CHAPTER 8

Human Rights
in Iran Today

As the persistent titleholder of most executions per capita in the world, it is no easy feat to articulate the unrestrained political, personal, legal, and human rights violations that define the Iranian regime's ruling apparatus today. Nearly any detail, minor or otherwise, of a typical Iranian's day-to-day life, reflects in some way the denial of basic and fundamental rights and liberties, relative to the rest of the developed world. A seemingly bottomless pit of transgressions exposes the inhuman treatment of Iran's people, primarily the absence of religious, judicial, and legal freedoms.

Iran's casual implementation of the death penalty is ironic, given the stringent and lengthy list of offenses that land one in jail. Of the more than 450 executions that took place from January through September 2017, many victims were drug addicts and substance abusers. Whereas other countries of the developed or western world dedicate or at the very least advocate substance abuse programs and state-run rehab initiatives, Iran elects to kill off its citizens who fall victim to drug abuse, regardless of extenuating circumstances. The caveat here is that it is the Islamic Revolutionary Guard Corps (IRGC) that runs a major part of the narcotics trafficking in Iran, generating huge profits, which the IRGC uses for its extraterritorial activities.

Moreover, virtually all of these executions are in contravention of internationally-recognized standards, such as the presumption of innocence, access to lawyers, public trials, and due process. Those not being executed for drug offenses are often given the death penalty for other, ordinary offenses, often alleged after subjecting the victims to vicious tortures to extract concessions.

As confirmed by previous UN investigators on Iran's human rights record, many dissidents have been executed on the pretext of committing crimes such as drug trafficking. Of course, the regime has never been hesitant about executing its opponents, sometimes *en masse* on security related charges, whether they be activists of the principal opposition movement, the People's Mojahedin Organization of Iran (PMOI/MEK), or dissident ethnic minorities, such as the Kurds, Baluchis, or Arabs. Adherents of other faiths are not spared either. Dozens of Sunnis, Christians, Bahai's, and others have also been given the death penalty.

Contrary to its Citizen Rights Charter, Iranians apparently do not have a right to life.

The current official age at which execution is permissible is nine lunar years for a girl, and 15 lunar years for a boy. The idea of executing a 9-year-old female or 15-year-old male conflicts with every international standard and ethics code known to the free world, but according to Iranian regime's legal code, it is justified. From January to September of 2017, the executions involved at least four victims who were minors at the time of their arrests. In many cases, victims are held in prison until they reach 18 years of age, when they are then executed.

When it comes to capital punishment in Iran, there are all sorts of jaw-dropping exceptions to international norms. It is safe to assume that so long as a murder is supplemented with justification by *shari'a* law, in one way or another, the act is excused. In Iran, for example, stoning and honor killings are excusable if they involve a woman.

The denial of basic rights to women affects all aspects of public and private life. Should a woman enter a public space without *hijab*, or proper covering, a possible consequence will involve her being lashed — dozens of times, depending on the "severity" of the "crime." A woman can be pulled over while driving or walking, if an agent views her *hijab* as not properly covering her. Wardrobe malfunctions can have much more disturbing consequences. In 2014 in Isfahan, sporadic "acid attacks" began all over the city, when self-appointed vigilantes associated with the paramilitary *Bassij* force splashed acid into the faces of women deemed inappropriately covered. A number of these women went blind from the attacks. While the actions were not officially claimed by the regime, officials did nothing to seriously investigate these vicious assaults and no one was arrested or prosecuted, further convincing the public that the government had sanctioned the attacks.

Iranian women have little representation in government, are second-hand citizens and under the current legal code, have no hopes for improvement. They are subject to discrimination as trivial as being banned from attending official sporting matches, and are barred from practicing sports unless dressed in full *hijab*. According to the October 2017 Report of the Secretary General, in February 2017, a chess player was banned from competing in domestic tournaments because she had reportedly appeared at a competition without a headscarf. In April, the Iranian Futsal Federation expelled a female player from the national team after finding a picture of her playing without a headscarf on social media.

This maltreatment paints a vivid picture of the attributes women are forced to adopt: submission, silence, and obedience. Women in Iran are resilient, nevertheless, and many have fought back. Citing the Secretary General's Report, in 2017, none of the 137 women who put their name forward to run for president passed the vetting by the Guardian Council. Consequently, there were no women candidates in the presidential elections. Further, no women have been appointed as ministers in Rouhani's new cabinet.

Securing data about the situation of women and human rights in general is itself a daunting task. Journalists are no safer than women in their day-to-day endeavors. Should the facts and opinions journalists disseminate be at "odds" with the regime's official version, journalists, bloggers, and social media activists risk arrest and even execution. Freedom of expression and opinion is harshly suppressed. In the weeks and months preceding a national election, the crackdown on dissident opinions can be particularly severe. Whether ordinary citizens using illegal platforms like Facebook or Twitter to broadcast unorthodox ideas, or established journalist publishing data or stories that paint the regime in an unflattering light, risk punitive reprisals. The regime can shut down whatever newspaper, magazine, website, or social media account it deems responsible for advocating peaceful protests or thought-provoking ideas. The Iranian regime both directly and indirectly, controls and signs off on every television program, magazine article, and news broadcast.

These are just a few of the acts that will result in torturous intimidation in Iran. Floggings are on the milder side of the spectrum. A citizen may receive a flogging for offenses such as breaking fast in public during Ramadan, accessing websites or social media platforms that are "forbidden," publishing false news (the key word being "false," of course, which is at the discretion of the government), and criticizing government officials.

The regime also regularly responds to disobedience –both when the offense occurs in public or the citizen is in government detention—with amputations, blinding, eye-gouging, and public executions. This cruel method of death is one of the most inhumane ways to end someone's life.

Publicizing executions is intended to intimidate the masses, making them afraid of expressing their views and their opposition to the regime. Interestingly, the so-called moderate president Hassan Rouhani is on record as saying that people should be hanged in public to make examples out of them for other citizens. "Conspirators should be hanged in Friday prayers for people to see them and to have more of an impact," he said when he was a parliament deputy. The preferred method of spotlighting capital punishment is public hangings from cranes in city centers.

The real takeaway, though, is not necessarily that the government responds to offenses with harsh, brutal physical retaliation. While gouging its own citizens' eyes out, or blinding or amputating them, or executing them in public is horrendous, what truly stands out are the "offenses" that "warrant" such responses. Citizens cannot express politically incorrect opinions, cannot criticize government officials, and live in fear of violating what the regime deems "appropriate." Meanwhile, the regime strives to represent itself as "democratic" to the rest of the world. "Elections" are held among candidates exclusively chosen by the ayatollahs, and then rigged.

Despite the regime's four decades of brutal reprisals, intended to repress its population of over 80 million people, the majority of Iranians are under the age of 30, and are incorrigibly eager to express their opinions, voice their outrage, and, above all else, facilitate change within their country.

CHAPTER 9
The Way Forward

Though Iran's pattern of executions and human rights violations continues today, it is clear that the regime has been weakened on the subject, rendering the present moment as a turning point in the fortunes of the Iranian people. With the release of the Montazeri tape in the summer of 2016, government officials responsible for the 1988 massacre were forced to admit their guilt. Though they initially attempted to cover up their actions, the world is now aware of the role that each perpetrator played in the injustices of 1988. This revelation opens the door for a way forward in Iran.

On the twenty-ninth anniversary of the 1988 massacre, Iranian opposition leader Maryam Rajavi gave a speech entitled "The Campaign for Justice Has Shaken the Reign of Terror," describing the horrors of the "summer of blood" and outlining the actions she believed Iranians should take in order to expand the movement. Rajavi described the ways in which the Iranian opposition had been successful in pressuring the regime into action and acknowledgement of its crimes. She praised the efforts of Iranian activists thus far, but noted that "Despite all that has been done so far, this is still only the first step. The Iranian people and Resistance will not sit back until the perpetrators of the 1988 massacre of political prisoners, many of whom currently hold key positions in the government, are brought to justice." Mrs. Rajavi emphasized that the achievements of the opposition up to this point should serve as a springboard for future movements and urged members to push even harder for justice.

Many important steps have been taken on the path to justice in Iran. However, there is still no accountability amongst members of the regime. Though there is damning evidence against many current government officials, several of whom have admitted their guilt, the perpetrators of the 1988 massacre remain in power today. It is also apparent that the violent practices of Iran continue unabated. Iran remains the country with the most executions per-capita, and is the only nation in the world that still executes juvenile prisoners. The regime continues to imprison and kill political prisoners simply because of their alleged affiliations with the MEK, and almost always fails to give them fair trials. Governments, officials, and organizations worldwide have spoken out about and called for the end of the unjust practices, from Hillary Clinton to Amnesty International. It is clear that there is widespread consensus on the matter of human rights in Iran, with a variety of groups being united against the crimes of the regime.

Another crucial injustice is the lack of information regarding the victims of the 1988 massacre. While the regime has acknowledged the occurrence of the killings, very little is known about the victims and the location of their bodies. The graves and names of the victims, which have long been shrouded in secrecy by the Iranian government, must be released to the victims' families in order to bring closure. The names of the perpetrators of the massacre, some of which have been revealed over the course of the last two years, must also be revealed to the public to facilitate justice and accountability.

The way forward certainly involves holding the regime accountable for not only its past crimes against humanity, but its current violations as well. The people of Iran have made their voices heard and have produced results, but must continue to push for justice now more than ever. Youth and students in Iran have also had a significant impact on the nation's policy, and Mrs. Rajavi called upon them to continue protesting and fighting for transparency.

Governments and organizations must condemn the regime to an even greater degree. Verbal disapproval is not enough to halt the nefarious deeds that have been carried out over the last several decades; only financial or political repercussions can truly make a difference. The U.S. government has recently placed and expanded sanctions on the IRGC and its affiliates, which will have a serious impact on the regime's financial abilities. It is actions like these that must be taken against the Iranian government in order to bring about the change that is necessary.

Finally and perhaps most importantly, the massacre of 1988 must be thoroughly investigated by the United Nations. The international community should join together to hold the Iranian government accountable for the killing of 30,000 political prisoners, which amounts to a crime against humanity. Members of the regime have acknowledged both that the massacre occurred and admitted their role in the "summer of blood," paving the way for a UN response. Other political killings have been investigated by international communities in the past,[127] upholding justice and accountability

127 Blackwell, Ken. "Investigation of Argentina's 'Dirty War' Set Precedent for Inquiry into Iran's 'Summer of Blood.' TownHall, October 6, 2017. https://townhall.com/columnists/

while bringing closure to the families of the thousands of victims. The same must be done in Iran—it is high time that the call for justice in Iran be answered with tangible international force. The regime will not halt its illegal and violent practices without such drastic action.

APPENDIX A
Letters and Translations

Montazeri's first letter to Khomeini

بسم الله الرحمن الرحیم

محضر مبارک آیة الله العظمی امام خمینی مدظله العالی

پس از سلام و تحیت بعرض میرساند راجع به دستور اخیر حضرتعالی مبنی بر اعدام منافقین موجود در زندانها اعدام بازداشت شدگان حادثه اخیر را ملت و جامعه پذیرا است و ظاهراً اثر سوئی ندارد ولی اعدام موجودین از سابق در زندانها اولاً در شرایط فعلی حمل بر کینه توزی و انتقامجوئی میشود. و ثانیاً خانواده های بسیاری را که نوعاً متدین و انقلابی هستند ناراحت و داغدار میکند و از نظام دلزده میشوند. و ثالثاً بسیاری از آنان سرموضع نیستند ولی بعضی از مسئولین تند با آنان معامله سرموضع میکنند. و رابعاً در شرایط فعلی که با فشارها و حملات اخیر صدام و منافقین ما در دنیا چهره مظلوم بخود گرفته ایم و بسیاری از رسانه ها و شخصیتها از ما دفاع میکنند صلاح نظام و حضرتعالی نیست که یکدفعه تبلیغات علیه ما شروع شود. و خامساً افرادی که بوسیله دادگاهها با موازینی در سابق محکوم بکمتر از اعدام شده اند اعدام کردن آنان بدون مقدمه و بدون فعالیت تازه ای بی اعتنائی به همه موازین قضائی و احکام قضات است و عکس العمل خوب ندارد. و سادساً مسئولین قضائی و دادستانی و اطلاعات ما در سطح مقدس اردبیلی نیستند و اشتباهات و تحت تأثیر قرار گرفتنها بسیار زیاد و فراوان است و با حکم اخیر حضرتعالی بسا بیگناهان یا کم گناهانی هم اعدام میشوند و در امور مهمه اقدام هم منجر است. و سابعاً ما تاکنون از کشتنها و خشونتها نتیجه ای نگرفته ایم جز اینکه تبلیغات را علیه خود زیاد کرده ایم و جاذبه منافقین و ضد انقلاب را بیشتر نموده ایم بجاست مدتی با رحمت و عطوفت برخورد شود که قطعاً برای بسیاری جاذبه خواهد داشت. و ثامناً اگر فرضاً بر دستور خودتان اصرار دارید اقلاً دستور دهید ملاک اتفاق نظر قاضی و دادستان و مسئول اطلاعات باشد نه اکثریت و زنان هم مستثنی شوند مخصوصاً زنان بچه دار و بالاخره اعدام چند هزار نفر در ظرف چند روز هم عکس العمل خوب ندارد و هم خالی از خطا نخواهد بود. و بعضی از قضاة متدین بسیار ناراحت بودند و بجاست این حدیث شریف مورد توجه واقع شود: در قال رسول الله (ص): ادرؤا الحدود عن المسلمین ما استطعتم فان کان له مخرج فخلوا سبیله فان الامام ان یخطی فی العفو خیر من ان یخطی فی العقوبة. والسلام علیکم و ادام الله ظلکم ۱۶ ذی الحجه ۱۴۰۸ - ۶۷/۵/۹

The following is the full translation of Montazeri's letter:

Date: July 31, 1988

In the Name of God, the Compassionate, the Merciful,

His Exalted Eminence Imam Khomeini,

With greetings, I would like to apprise Your Eminence that following your recent decree for the execution of the Monafeqin [Mojahedin] who remain in prisons, the nation tolerates the execution of the detainees of recent events and they apparently have no adverse consequences, but the execution of those who were already in prison has the following consequences:

These executions are perceived as an act of vengeance and a vendetta, considering the present state of affairs;

Many families, even those who are pious and revolutionary, are distressed and aggrieved by these executions, and have turned their backs to our regime;

Many of the prisoners who are not holding fast to their views are being treated by the officials as if they were;

At a time when under the attacks and pressures of Saddam and the Monafeqin [Mojahedin], we are attracting some sympathy around the world and many newspapers and personalities are defending us, it is unwise for the regime and yourself to have the propaganda turn against us;

While these people have been sentenced by our courts to prison terms, to execute them without any process and new activity is a complete disregard for all judicial standards and judges' rulings. This will not reflect well on our regime;

Our judicial officials, prosecutors and intelligence officials are not perfect and there is plenty of opportunity for mistakes and unduly influenced decisions. With Your Eminence's recent decree, many people who have light charges or are innocent are executed;

We have not so far benefited from these killings and violence. We have only stirred more propaganda against ourselves and we have increased the appeal of the Monafeqin [Mojahedin] and the counter-revolutionaries. It is appropriate to treat them with mercy for a time so as to attract the sympathies of many of them;

If you insist on your decree, then at least issue an order so that the judge, the prosecutor and the intelligence official would have to reach a consensus for execution. They must particularly spare women with children. The execution of several thousand prisoners in a few days will not have positive repercussions and will not be mistake-free. Even some of our religious judges were very distressed by this.

Hossein-Ali Montazeri

Montazeri's second letter to Khomeini

The following is the full translation of his second letter:

Date: August 4, 1988

In the Name of God, the Compassionate, the Merciful,

His Exalted Eminence Imam Khomeini,

With greetings, pursuant to my letter of July 31, 1988, I write the following out of my sense of religious duty: Three days ago, a religious judge from one of the provinces, who is a trustworthy man, came to see me in Qom and was in great distress because of the way Your Eminence's decree is being implemented.

He said: The intelligence chief or the prosecutor (I forget which) was trying to ascertain if a prisoner was still holding fast to his beliefs.

He asked the prisoner if he was prepared to condemn the Monafeqin [Mojahedin], he said yes.

He asked him: 'Are you willing to go to the front to fight in the war with Iraq?' He said, 'Yes.'

They asked, 'Are you willing to walk over mines?' He said, 'Do you mean all the people are willing to walk over mines? Moreover, you must not have such high expectations from someone who has just changed his views.' They said, 'It is obvious that you are still holding on to your political beliefs,' and dealt with him in the same way they dealt with those who had held onto their previous political positions (and executed him)."

The judge told me how much he insisted that the verdict be issued by consensus, or a majority, but this was not accepted, because it is the intelligence official who has absolute control and others are under his influence.

Your Eminence can see what type of persons are implementing your grave decree that affects the lives of thousands of prisoners.

Hossein-Ali Montazeri

Montazeri's letter to Death Committee

بسمه تعالی

تاریخ ۶۷/۵/۲۴

شماره ....

خطاب به آقایان نیری، اشراقی، رئیسی و پورمحمدی

۱- من بیش از همه شما از منافقین ضربه خورده‌ام چه در زندان و چه در خارج زندان - فرزندم را آنان به شهادت رساندند - اگر بنا بر انتقام‌جویی باشد من بیشتر باید دنبال کنم ولی من مصلحت اسلام و انقلاب و کشور و حیثیت ولایت فقیه و حکومت اسلام را در نظر میگیرم من قضاوت آیندگان و تاریخ را در نظر میگیرم.

۲- این گونه قتل عام بدون محاکمه آن هم نسبت به زندانی و اسیر قطعاً در درازمدت به نفع آنها است و دنیا ما را محکوم میکند و آنان را بیشتر به مبارزه مسلحانه تشویق میکند مبارزه با فکر و ایده از طریق کشتن غلط است

۳- روش پیغمبر را با دشمنان خود در فتح مکه و جنگ هوازن ببینید به چه نحو بوده است پیغمبر با عفو و اغماض برخورد کرد و از خداوند عنوان رحمة للعالمین گرفت روش امیرالمؤمنین با اهل جمل را پس از شکست آنان ملاحظه کنید

۴- بسیاری از افراد سر موضع را فشار و برخورد زندانبانان آنان را سر موضع کرده والا قبلاً انعطاف داشته‌اند

۵- مجرد اینکه اگر آنان را آزاد کنیم به منافقین ملحق میشوند موجب صدق عنوان محارب و باغی بر آنان نمیشود امیرالمؤمنین نسبت به ابن‌ملجم هم قبل از جنایت اقدام نکرد با اینکه خودش خبر داد او قاتل من است

۶- مجرد اعتقاد فرد را داخل عنوان محارب و باغی نمیکند و ارتداد سران فرضاً موجب حکم به ارتداد سمپاتها نمیشود

۷- قضاوت و حکم باید در جو سالم و خالی از احساسات باشد (لا یقضی القاضی و هو غضبان) الآن با شعارها و تحریکات جو ناسالم است ما از جنایت منافقین در غرب ناراحتیم بجان اسرا و زندانیان سابق افتاده‌ایم و انگهی اعدام آنان بدون فعالیت جدید زیر سؤال بردن همه قضات و همه قضاوتهای سابق است کسی را که به کمتر از اعدام محکوم کرده‌اید به چه ملاک اعدام میکنید.

۸- اینجانب از همه بیشتر نگران حیثیت حضرت امام و وجهه ولایت فقیه می‌باشم و نمی‌دانم موضوع را به چه نحوی به اطلاع ایشان رسانده‌اند این همه ما در فقه گفتیم احتیاط در دماء و اموال و استدلال کردیم همه غلط بود؟

۹- من چندین نفر از قضات عاقل و متدین را دیدم که ناراحت بودند و از نحوه اجرا شکایت داشتند و میگفتند تندروی میشود و نمونه‌های زیادی را ذکر میکردند که بی‌جهت حکم اعدام اجرا شده

۱۰- در خاتمه مجاهدین خلق اشخاص نیستند یک سنخ فکر و برداشت است یک نوع منطق است منطق غلط را باید با منطق صحیح جواب داد با کشتن حل نمیشود بلکه ترویج میشود ان‌شاءالله موفق باشید ح-م.

[illegible]

The following is the full translation of Montazeri's letter to the Death Committee:

To Mr. Nayyeri, [religious judge], Mr. Eshraqi, [prosecutor], Mr. Raissi, [deputy prosecutor], and Mr. Pourmohammadi, [Intelligence Ministry representative]

Date: August 15, 1988

In the Name of God, the Most High,

1. I have received more blows from the Monafeqin [Mojahedin] than all of you, both in prison and outside.

My son was martyred by them. If it was a question of revenge, I should pursue it more than you. But I seek the expediency and interests of the revolution, Islam, the Supreme Leader, and the Islamic state. I am worried about the judgment that posterity and history will pass upon us.

2. Such massacres without trial, particularly when the victims are prisoners and those in captivity, will definitely benefit them in the long run. The world will condemn us and they will be further encouraged to wage armed struggle. It is wrong to confront ideas and ideologies with killings.

3. Look at the behavior of Prophet [Mohammad] and how he treated his enemies after the conquest of Mecca and the Battle of Hawazen. The Prophet showed mercy and amnesty and was given the title of "the Mercy of both worlds" by the Almighty. Look how Imam Ali treated his enemies after defeating them in the Battle of Jamal.

4. Many of these people who are holding fast to their beliefs are doing so in reaction to the way they have been treated by interrogators and prison wardens, otherwise they might have been flexible.

5. To argue that if we released these prisoners, they would rejoin the Monafeqin [Mojahedin] is not sufficient to characterize them as Mohareb (waging war on God) and of having mutinied against God. Imam Ali did not punish Ibn Moljem (his assassin), before he actually carried out the crime, even though he said before hand that he (Ibn Moljem) is my killer....

6. The beliefs of a person, per se, are not sufficient grounds to

declare him as someone who is waging war on God or rebelling against the Almighty. Even if it is supposed that the [Mojahedin] leaders are renegades, their supporters cannot be given the same verdict.

7. Judgment must be made in an environment free of emotions. The social environment now is not conducive to justice due to sloganeering and propaganda. We are upset with the Monafeqin's crime in the west, but are taking it out on prisoners and former prisoners. Executing people who have not carried out any new activities will cast doubt on previous judges and all previous judgments. According to which standard do you execute a prisoner whom you have previously given a lesser sentence? At present, prison visits and telephone calls have been cut off, but how will you answer the families tomorrow?

8. I, more than anybody, care about the prestige of His Eminence the Imam as the Supreme Leader. I do not know how things are being presented to him. Should we say that all that we were studying in Islamic jurisprudence about taking caution when dealing with people's blood and properties were wrong?

9. I have met with a number of just and pious judges who were dismayed and complained about the way the decree is being implemented. They said there is too much extremism and cited numerous cases of people being executed without any reason.

10. In conclusion, the People's Mojahedin are not individuals; they are an ideology, and a world outlook. They have a logic. It takes right logic to answer wrong logic. You cannot rectify wrong with killings; you only spread it.

Hossein-Ali Montazeri

Khomeini's letter to Montazeri dismissing him as his successor

Khomeini reacted sharply and in a letter dismissed Mr. Montazeri as his designated successor.

Khomeini openly accused Montazeri of paving the way for the main opposition PMOI (MEK) to take over the country. The letter is yet another proof of the fact that Khomeini was behind all the suppressive measures and justified them under the name of Islam and God.

Translation of Khomeini's letter to Montazeri dismissing him of his successor:

In the name of God, the Merciful, the Compassionate.

To Mr. Montazeri.

My heart is broken and filled with blood now that I am writing a few words to you. Perhaps one day the people will realize the facts by reading this letter.

In your recent letter to me, you said that, in accordance with the Shari'ah, you give priority to my views over your own. I consider God my witness when I point out the following issues:

Since it has become clear that after me you are going to hand over this country, our dear Islamic revolution, and the Muslim people of Iran to the liberals, and through that channel to the Hypocrites [Mojahedin-e Khalq], you are no longer eligible to succeed me as the legitimate leader of the state. You, in most of your letters, speeches and stances, have shown that you believe the liberals and Hypocrites should rule this country. It is so clear that your remarks have been dictated by the Hypocrites that I did not see any point in sending a reply. For instance, thanks to your speeches and written work, the Hypocrites took advantage of your stance in defense of their ilk to promote a number of their comrades—who had been condemned to death on charges of waging an armed struggle against Islam and the revolution—to positions of authority. Can you see what valuable services you have offered to arrogance? On the issue of the murderer Mahdi Hashemi [a supporter and relative of Ayatollah Montazeri, who was later executed], you considered him to be the most religious person on earth. Despite the fact that it was proved to you that he was a murderer, you kept sending messages to me to spare his life. There are so many other examples, similar to that of Mahdi Hashemi, that I cannot be bothered to mention them all.

You no longer have the power of attorney on my behalf. Tell the people who bring you gold and money to take them to Mr. Pasandideh's [Khomeini's elder brother] residence in Qom or to me in Jamaran. Praise be to God, you yourself will not have any financial commitments from this date.

If, in accordance with the Shari'ah, you do consider my views to be superior to yours (which certainly the Hypocrites will advise you that it is against your interests to do so; and no doubt you will become busy writing things which will further deteriorate your future), then you should listen to the following words of advice I am giving you. It breaks my heart and my chest is full of agonizing pain when I see that you, the fruit of my life's labor, are so ungrateful. However, by relying on Almighty God, I give you the following words of advice, and it will be up to you whether you take note of them or not:

One: Try to change the members of your cabinet so as to avoid feeding the hypocrites, Mahdi Hashemi's clique, and the liberals from the sacred charity funds donated to the Imam.

Two: Since you are a gullible [sadeh lowh] person and are provoked easily, do not interfere in political matters, and maybe then God will forgive you for your sins.

Three: Do not write to me ever again, and do not allow the hypocrites to pass state secrets to foreign radio stations.

Four: Since you became a mouthpiece of the Hypocrites and your speeches have conveyed their wishes to the people via the mass media, you have inflicted heavy blows on Islam and the revolution. This is a great act of treason against the unknown soldiers of the Lord of the Age, may our souls be sacrificed for him, and against the sacrifices made by the illustrious martyrs of Islam and the revolution. If you wish to save yourself from hell fire, you had better confess to all your sins and mistakes and maybe then God will help you.

I swear to God that from the start I was against choosing you as my successor, but at the time I did not realize you were so gullible. To me you were not a resourceful manager but an educated person who could benefit the religious seminaries. If you continue your deeds I will definitely be obliged to do something about you. And you know me, I never neglect my obligation. I swear to God that I was against appointing Mahdi Bazargan as the first prime minister, too, but I considered him to be a decent person. I also swear to God that I did not vote for Bani-Sadr as the president either. On all these occasions I submitted to the advice of my friends. In the midst of my pain and suffering, I wish to address our dear people from the bottom of my broken heart:

I have made a pledge to my God not to forgive evil individuals ever, if I am not obliged to do so. I have made a pledge to my God that pleasing Him [God] is a much greater priority than pleasing my friends and other people. If the entire world were to rise against me, I would never abandon justice and the truth. I do not care about history and current developments. I am only interested in performing my religious duties. In addition to my pledge to God, I have promised the decent, noble, and honest people to inform them of the facts when the time is appropriate. Islam's history is full of instances of treason by its prominent figures against Islam. Try to make sure that you are not influenced by the lies broadcast by foreign radio stations. These radio stations dictate their lies with so much joy and enthusiasm these days. I beseech Almighty God to grant patience and tolerance to this old father of the dear Iranian people. I beseech God to forgive me and to take me away from this world so that I no longer have to experience the bitter taste of my friend's treachery. We all submit to God's will. We have no power without God's will. Everything comes from Him.

Wishing you peace: Ruhollah al-Musavi al-Khomeini; dated: Sunday 6 Farvardin 1368. (26 March 1989)

APPENDIX B
List of Publications

List of Publications by the National Council of Resistance of Iran, U.S. Representative Office

Iran's Nuclear Core: Uninspected Military Sites, Vital to the Nuclear Weapons Program

October 2017, 52 pages

This book details how the nuclear weapons program is at the heart, and not in parallel, to the civil nuclear program of Iran. The program has been run by the Islamic Revolutionary Guards Corp (IRGC) since the beginning, and the main nuclear sites and nuclear research facilities have been hidden from the eyes of the United Nations nuclear watchdog.

Terrorist Training Camps in Iran: How Islamic Revolutionary Guards Corps Trains Foreign Fighters to Export Terrorism

June 1017, 56 pages

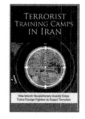

The book details how Islamic Revolutionary Guards Corps trains foreign fighters in 15 various camps in Iran to export terrorism. The IRGC has created a large directorate within its extraterritorial arm, the Quds Force, in order to expand its training of foreign mercenaries as part of the strategy to step up its meddling abroad in Syria, Iraq, Yemen, Bahrain, Afghanistan and elsewhere.

Presidential Elections in Iran: Changing Faces; Status Quo Policies

May 2017, 78 pages

The book, reviews the past 11 presidential elections, demonstrating that the only criterion for qualifying as a candidate is practical and heartfelt allegiance to the Supreme Leader. An unelected vetting watchdog, the Guardian Council makes that determination.

The Rise of Iran's Revolutionary Guards' Financial Empire: How the Supreme Leader and the IRGC Rob the People to Fund International Terror

March 2017, 174 pages

This manuscript examines some vital factors and trends, including the overwhelming and accelerating influence (especially since 2005) of the Supreme Leader and the Islamic Revolutionary Guard Corps (IRGC). This study shows how ownership of property in various spheres of the economy is gradually shifted from the population writ large towards a minority ruling elite comprised of the Supreme Leader's office and the IRGC, using 14 powerhouses, and how the money ends up funding terrorism worldwide.

How Iran Fuels Syria War: Details of the IRGC Command HQ and Key Officers in Syria

November 2016, 74 pages

This book examines how the Iranian regime has effectively engaged in the military occupation of Syria by marshaling 70,000 forces, including the Islamic Revolutionary Guard Corps (IRGC) and mercenaries from other countries into Syria; is paying monthly salaries to over 250,000 militias and agents to prolong the conflict; divided the country into 5 zones of conflict and establishing 18 command, logistics and operations centers.

Nowruz 2016 with the Iranian Resistance: Hoping for a New Day, Freedom and Democracy in Iran

April 2016, 36 pages

This book describes Iranian New Year, Nowruz celebrations at the Washington office of Iran's parliament-in-exile, the National Council of Resistance of Iran. The yearly event marks the beginning of spring. It includes select speeches by dignitaries who have attended the NCRIUS Nowruz celebrations. This book also discusses the very rich culture and the traditions associated with Nowruz for centuries.

The 2016 Vote in Iran's Theocracy: An analysis of Parliamentary & Assembly of Experts Elections

February 2016, 70 pages

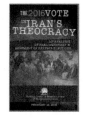

This book examines all the relevant data about the 2016 Assembly of Experts as well as Parliamentary elections ahead of the February 2016 elections. It looks at the history of elections since the revolution in 1979 and highlights the current intensified infighting among the various factions of the Iranian regime.

IRAN: A Writ of Deception and Cover-up: Iranian Regime's Secret Committee Hid Military Dimensions of its Nuclear Program

February 2016, 30 pages

The book provides details about a top-secret committee in charge of forging the answers to the International Atomic Energy Agency (IAEA) regarding the Possible Military Dimensions (PMD) of Tehran's nuclear program, including those related to the explosive detonators called EBW (Exploding Bridge Wire) detonator, which is an integral part of a program to develop an implosion type nuclear device.

Iranian Regime's Nuclear Duplicity: An Analysis of Tehran's Trickery in Talks with the P 5+1

January 2016, 74 pages

This book examines Iran's behavior throughout the negotiations process in an effort to inform the current dialogue on a potential agreement. Drawing on both publicly available sources and those within Iran, the book focuses on two major periods of intense negotiations with the regime: 2003-2004 and 2013-2015. Based on this evidence, it then extracts the principles and motivations behind Tehran's approach to negotiations as well as the tactics used to trick its counterparts and reach its objectives.

Key to Countering Islamic Fundamentalism: Maryam Rajavi's Testimony To The U.S. House Foreign Affairs Committee

June 2015, 68 pages

Testimony before U.S. House Foreign Affairs Committee's subcommittee on Terrorism, non-Proliferation, and Trade discussing ISIS and Islamic fundamentalism. The book contains Maryam Rajavi's full testimony as well as the question and answer by representatives.

Meet the National Council of Resistance of Iran

June 2014, 150 pages

Meet the National Council of Resistance of Iran discusses what NCRI stands for, what its platform is, what it has done so far, and why a vision for a free, democratic, secular, non-nuclear republic in Iran would serve the world peace.

How Iran Regime Cheated the World: Tehran's
Systematic Efforts to Cover Up its Nuclear Weapons Program

June 2014, 50 pages

This book deals with one of the most fundamental challenges that goes to the heart of the dispute regarding the Iranian regime's controversial nuclear program: to ascertain with certainty that Tehran will not pursue a nuclear bomb. Such an assurance can only be obtained through specific steps taken by Tehran in response to the international community's concerns. The monograph discusses the Iranian regime's report card as far as it relates to being transparent when addressing the international community's concerns about the true nature and the ultimate purpose of its nuclear program.

APPENDIX C
About NCRI-US

About NCRI-US

National Council of Resistance of Iran-US Representative Office acts as the Washington office for Iran's Parliament-in-exile, which is dedicated to the establishment of a democratic, secular, non-nuclear republic in Iran.

NCRI-US, registered as a non-profit tax-exempt organization, has been instrumental in exposing the nuclear weapons program of Iran, including the sites in Natanz, and Arak, the biological and chemical weapons program of Iran, as well as its ambitious ballistic missile program.

NCRI-US has also exposed the terrorist network of the Iranian regime, including its involvement in the bombing of Khobar Towers in Saudi Arabia, the Jewish Community Center in Argentina, its fueling of sectarian violence in Iraq and Syria, and its malign activities in other parts of the Middle East.

Our office has provided information on the human rights violations in Iran, extensive anti-government demonstrations, and the movement for democratic change in Iran.

Visit our website at **www.ncrius.org**

You may follow us on twitter 🐦 @ncrius

Follow us on ⓕ **facebook** NCRIUS

You can also find us on 📷 *Instagram* NCRIUS

CPSIA information can be obtained
at www.ICGtesting.com
Printed in the USA
FSOW03n2034301117
41572FS